IN PRAISE

G000077082

Hear Your Heart Whisper from the Stillness is necessary reading for the time we live in. Nancy Smyth's accessible and joyous teachings, poems, and meditations encourage us, no matter where or who we are, to slow down and find quiet within ourselves and from that place, expansiveness abounds. To read this book is like experiencing a moving meditation - enjoy it in full and know you can return to moments that call to you time and time again.

> Sullivan Whitely
> Operations at Chief

Nancy Smyth brings her calming wisdom straight to your heart with this gentle book, with a serenity that happifies the soul.

> Jim Ferrell
> Founder at Withii Leadership Center
> Bestselling Author

Experiencing *Hear Your Heart Whisper from the Stillness* is like reveling in gentle ocean waves that quietly wash over you. Wisdom is simply shared, and it calls you to stop and reflect on what is most important in life. Thomas Merton once said, "There is no way of telling people that they are walking around like the sun." I believe that Nancy has found a way to reveal a few rays of that sunlight to her readers.

There is much to savor between the pages of this book. I encourage you to dive in!

> Sr. Maureen Fitzgerald, ascj
> Learning Consultant

This is a beautiful book. It invites you to explore your heart and the beauty within. It's not a book "about the heart." It's a book that is written from the heart and takes you directly into your own heart.

Sarah McCrum

Author of *Love Money, Money Loves You*

Podcast: The Spirit of Business

Nancy's love of people and their success makes her a not-to-be-missed companion on your heart's journey through life. In this book, she takes us on a new adventure. Her presence is delightfully tranquil while being powerfully transformative.

Chuck Pettet

Commodities Trader

Nancy has created a transformational book. (Note the key difference between information and transformation.) Yes, there is excellent information, using great teachings, storytelling, poetry, and hands-on exercises. However, as I turned these pages, I felt more connected and alive. The book had me genuinely look deep into my mind, heart, and soul as to the life I desire to live.

Hear Your Heart Whisper from the Stillness is for the person who wants to slow down and look within - truly design life from a whole new paradigm....and to be quite honest, I dare say who doesn't want that!

Nancy's words create internal experiences that open up ways of being and doing that truly change your game.

Rick Tamlyn

Hay House Author of *Play Your Bigger Game*

Master Certified Coach (ICF)

Senior trainer of The Co-Active Institute.

I first met Nancy after a sound healing experience I had created. She immediately came over to introduce herself and share her experience and feelings with me. It felt like we had known one another for many lifetimes and united again in this divine timing.

Her wealth of knowledge and intuition weave together to meet you where you are and support you on your journey. Encountering her in this book, you will fill with so much insight, pure love, and light.

Nancy is beyond kind and gifted; her book will revolutionize and transform your life.

Sugar Panbehchi
Creator of Be Crystal Clear (Mind, Body, Spirit Center)

Nancy's unique way of viewing life and the world, combined with her experience and insight, will point you in the direction of the extraordinary life that you want to live. Just as you would take someone's hand to help you climb a steep slope, let Nancy guide you.

Danny Iny
Founder/CEO at Mirasee
Recent books: *Teach Your Gift* | *Effortless* | *Online Courses*

In our chaotic, noisy world, this book is a great distillation of life wisdom that will guide you to inner tranquility and clarity so you can show up with greater flexibility in the face of life's challenges. Interspersed with stories and poetry, reading this book is meditative and will put you in touch with your highest self.

I highly recommend it!

Bhoomi Pathak
COO at Mirasee

Ah, yes, Nancy Smyth. We first met over the phone 20 years ago. It was through her that I was introduced to the world of coaching. As a practicing therapist, I was intrigued by the coaching approach. We explored the application of principles from The Arbinger Institute with clients both at home and in the workplace.

But more importantly, over the next 18 years of working off and on with Nancy, I began to see the person she was. I recognized in her the authenticity, sincerity, transparency, and openness that so often eluded me. Nancy helped me see the place of peace that was waiting for me the more I "showed up" in any interaction.

Chris Wallace, LMFT, Ph.D.

Hear Your Heart Whisper from the Stillness brings you to the brink of self-discovery and masterful living in the modern age. This work is an evolutionary contribution to human understanding, as it speaks to the art and science of how to reach our human potential, using our own humanity as the compass. Nancy's writings are a lantern of wisdom illuminating the missing link for so many of us in this lifetime.

Nancy's book is soup for the soul.

Laurel Elders, PCC, CEC

Founder/CEO at The Institute for Integrative Intelligence®

One thing I have cherished about Nancy is how she is the personification of what she speaks. I have experienced (on multiple occasions) how her being completely peaceful has helped me do the same in that very moment!

Sucheth Davuluri

Vice Chairman of the Board/CEO at Neuland Laboratories Ltd.

In *Hear Your Heart Whisper from the Stillness*, Nancy A Smyth shares her invaluable wisdom, education, and life experience. Through her engaging storytelling and poetic writing style, she guides us to discover and listen to our deepest truth…our heart.

Specific tools, success formulas, and exercises offer an invitation to transform a life of struggle, heartache, and misery into extraordinary joy, wholehearted peace, and love!

I have incorporated these principles and tools in my 25-year coaching practice working with families and transforming corporate culture and educational organizations. They have been life-changing, for my clients and me. Thank you, Nancy, for this incredible gift!

Keri Maughan

Certified Life Coach (ICF)

Trainer

Founder at HeartSet fostering Compassion, Connection, Communication

Hear Your Heart Whisper from the Stillness

NANCY A SMYTH

Published by
Hybrid Global Publishing
301 E 57th Street
4th Floor
New York, NY 10022

Manufactured in the United States of America, or in the United Kingdom when distributed elsewhere.

Smyth, Nancy A
Hear Your Heart Whisper from the Stillness
LCCN: 2021907330
      ISBN: 978-1-951943-63-9
      eBook: 978-1-951943-64-6

Cover design by: Suzanne Oviedo and Joe Potter
Interior design by: Suzanne Oviedo and Suba Murugan
Copyediting by: Lara Kennedy
Poetry editing by: Barbara Daniels
Author photo by: Annie Gensheimer

TwoWiseWomen.org

CONTENTS

FOREWORD

You hold in your hands a treasure trove. I am so happy Nancy is able to share her vast experience and wisdom with a broad audience through this book.

I first met Nancy A Smyth many years ago when I was a student in her global course, The Choice in Coaching. The first thing I noticed was how Nancy held the space. Within seconds of being in the first session, I slowed down. She would ask a question that encouraged a long silence filled with reassurance and time to ponder. After getting over my initial surprise, I found it delicious. In those moments, I learned how to tap more into my heart space. That course transformed my life.

Years before I met her, Nancy studied with an Aztec medicine man, and I felt that being with her and learning from her was like visiting a tribal elder, someone with a deep understanding who has lived a long time and learned from experience.

I had the bounty of opportunity to partner with Nancy and coteach The Choice in Coaching, which we continued to do for more than a decade. The coursework was profound and brought up many deep questions for students. Before answering each inquiry, Nancy would pause, breathe, and listen to the whisperings from the stillness of her heart. Whatever flowed out from her helped a student go deeper. Her response often stunned me with its depth and resonance. Hundreds of students' hearts and lives changed completely.

In 2015, Nancy and I founded Two Wise Women, a coaching and training business that helps leaders thrive and prosper.

We coauthored *Chocolate or Lunch: How Choices Impact Relationships*. We work together almost every day—teaching many different courses, coaching, writing a blog, hosting a Facebook group. We bring laughter, joy, and insight to all we offer. *Hear Your Heart Whisper from the Stillness* embodies lessons learned and lived by Two Wise Women. I tell you all of this so you can trust me when I say:

To be with Nancy is a gift. You FEEL her presence. She brings her sharp mind, her open heart, and her uncanny intuitive powers to each moment.

Nancy is alive in this book. Read and reread it. Digest it. Practice what she suggests. If some parts don't make sense to your mind, listen with your heart. Let the energy of the stories and the poetic words seep under your skin. This book will transform you.

—Sharon Eakes

INTRODUCTION

Thank you for being here. I welcome you with all my heart.

Growing up, my life wasn't easy. My parents' continual fighting wreaked havoc on my siblings' and my emotions. One summer afternoon, I couldn't ingest any more abusive sounds. Grabbing my sunscreen, transistor radio, and blanket, I went outside to lie in the sun.

The sky was a beautiful blue, and even though I could still hear their warring, I was wrapped in the sun's warmth and feeling a sweet breeze blow through my hair. I could breathe.

At that moment, I felt sure: peace is possible. That is when I knew I was onto something. Love, peace, and joy became my North Star. With seasoned wisdom, I pass the benefits of starshine to you for your life.

Whatever our roles or status, we all want to belong, to experience happiness, contentment, and success. Our heart unfailingly lights the path to those extraordinary experiences. The focal point of this book will help us comprehend and activate all our heart's capacities. Knowing who we are and who we can become makes all the difference.

As I gathered my thoughts, I thought of you and the extraordinary life you wish to live. These pages will unfold boundless joy and contentment—brimming with love and kindness. Chapters clearly define core principles and lovingly prescribe a course of action that has been beneficial to both me and my clients.

Some chapters and reflections were written as responses to friends and clients. What they experienced, struggled with, and learned in their lives create an invaluable and sure pathway for us to traverse.

During my journey, I discovered the power of the human heart. I have also come to relish our phenomenal mind. We will penetrate both the heart's and mind's wisdom and see how, functioning together, they shine as one splendid light. We will merge them in profound partnership to lead us toward joy and success.

As we look through many lenses, the overlapping thoughts are positioned to clarify new questions that might surface.

Even though this book is not designed to be a primer, my intention has been to approach each topic so that newcomers can understand concepts and gain insights—fresh ways of seeing themselves and the world. In addition to the book offering knowledge and perhaps novel approaches to reality, its design helps return us to our natural, original state of love.

The lessons will get quite deep, quite fast. And chapters are purposely interspersed with reflective poetry and stories to help bypass the logical mind and stimulate pause, curiosity, and contemplation.

Here are a few suggestions to get the most from your read:

1. I use the words "people" and "others" throughout the book and invite you to consider everyone—no matter their age, closeness to you, or status—to belong to this category.
2. You are wholeheartedly encouraged to pause and engage with the information and digest it as you read. You can think of this time as an opportunity for advancement.
3. Try on everything to see what fits best. Explore your own being through self-reflection.

4. Enjoy the freedom you acquire from using your wisdom with and for others.

In following the guidance, you will never be heart-poor again.

Feel free to challenge or question the thoughts. I am happy to hear your opinions and look forward to growing with you.

A STORY

Once, a young man in India was suffering from health problems due to his love for sweets and sugar. His mother tried everything she knew to change his eating habits, but he could not, or would not, change. It seemed that the more she got after him, the worse his problem became.

Finally, at a loss for how to help him, she took him to see Gandhi, whom she knew her son admired. "Mahatma," she said upon reaching him, "my son is in ill health because of his love for sugar. Could you please tell him to stop eating sugar? Perhaps he would listen to you."

Gandhi paused for a moment, thinking. Then he looked at the woman and said, "Madame, bring your son back in three weeks. Then I will speak with him."

Three weeks later, the mother again traveled with her son to see Gandhi, whereupon he told the boy to stop eating sugar.

"Why did we have to wait three weeks for that?" the mother asked.

"Madame," Gandhi responded, "three weeks ago, I was still eating sugar."

—Source Unknown

THE GIFT

Why say I didn't expect this?
Why would I return it unused?
Why would I pretend it was not mine?

The gift—this life—my life
I am in it and need to pause, to ponder
Why?

Am I saying yes to step into the blazing fire of love—
to dismantle all between me and the flames,
to race with abandon, falling headlong into bright light,
fiery oceans of love.

Life shouts out eagerly, insistently—
accept and live
the life that only you can etch in time.

L O V E in capital letters
demands surrender.
Plunge your heart in devotion—
dissolve into the subtlest fragrance.

FROM MY HEART TO YOURS

Imagine a sublime potter expertly and affectionately shaping
a new creation, YOU
taking on form to set out on an extraordinary journey.
A unique earthenware shape that friends and family
delight in accompanying,
yet your journey to uncover precious treasure is taken alone.

It is a sacred trek, going deeper—and deeper—
leaving behind all shades of fear, doubt, illusion—
trembling, questioning yourself—
to find your glorious destiny of love and light.
Allow me to walk alongside,
to wipe away tearfulness, offer gifts of courage and love.

I will speak with you
of sacredness, of embracing your golden heart,
of honoring and washing away sorrows, resolving strife,
of enjoying sweet serenity and benevolence,
of infinite stillness, seemingly breathless,
silent, yet filled with vibrancy

Of an unerring path stretching out before you,
weaving through each cycle of life, seen or unseen,
ready to receive your blessed feet;
of trust for your path's enduring presence
leading you homeward;
of wakefulness and respect—

Of persistence to step back on course—
again—and again—and again,
growing just a little more resolute each time,
confident, wise—
traveling with hope
into astonishing worlds.

CHAPTER 1

Our Heart

There is a sacred temple in a sheltered, tranquil place. We dream of it, visit it from time to time, and ache to dwell in this most elusive and beautiful place.

We catch a glimpse of its joy when we fill to overflowing with laughter. We feel its expansiveness when we do the right thing, in the right way, at the right time. We encounter its splendid beauty when unconditional love pours through our bodies. We are awed by its brilliance while communing with nature. We sense its magic when we ask and have felt forgiveness. We hear it resound over and over when we wholeheartedly share the phrase *I love you*. We feel its fires burn in our belly when we fall to our knees in gratitude. These are exhilarating moments in our lives; they are full of blessings. They are a loving language of responses, communications, from the temple of our heart.

A thousand paths lead to the temple.
There we'll experience our pure essence,
delighting in who we genuinely are—
beauty, luminosity, goodness incarnate.

How do we have more of these experiences? How do we abide in the temple? We need to believe that the temple is ours, our birthright and our destiny. Once we make a conscious choice to live from our heart, the entryway opens before us. For many, it feels unlikely and perhaps an implausible journey to undertake. However, it is not as difficult as we imagine, and it is incredibly deserving of the effort.

Perhaps not experiencing yourself living fully inside the temple yet, you have worried. Is it possible? And can this truly exist for me?

Absolutely, and to get there is the most extraordinary exploration we will ever brave. It mandates taking a sacred pilgrimage.

HONORING OUR HEART

I am driving one early winter morning, not knowing that there is black ice on the two-lane hill I am descending. My car skids and turns sideways into oncoming traffic. Heart pounding—holding my breath—I clench the steering wheel tighter as my car spins out farther and slides off the road.

Stopped in a field. Collapsing—my head to the steering wheel, I let out a huge cry of relief and thanks—I am safe.

We are aware of our heart's role, how vital it is for physical, mental, and emotional health. What is not generally known is that the heart's pulsations are an intelligent language. Our heartbeats affect feelings, intuition, creativity, even cognition, and our physical well-being. Every organ in our body responds to, aligns with, and is enhanced by a heart at peace, a heart of joy, whereas, during that tense driving experience, my racing heart was broadcasting urgency.

Our heart's vibrations create our inner and outer worlds. Scientific research establishes that tranquil heartbeats boost all human functions and strengthen connection, harmony, and balance in the world we inhabit.

Spend a few moments now with your heart. If it is comfortable, you can place your hand or hands lightly on your chest over your heart. Pause and notice your heart's cadence. Thank your precious heart for its faithful service, devotion, astonishing beauty, innate guidance, and for the wonderful experiences it offers.

Relax your whole being. Imagine the breath entering your heart as you breathe. Inhale into your heart to a slow count of five, then calmly release the breath for a count of five—envision your breath snuggling the heart. Allow your heart to soften and expand. Linger here for a while longer, savoring gentle, deep breaths flowing in and out of your precious heart.

You are becoming aware of your own true self by slowing down and becoming focused on your heart—becoming more in tune with the pure pulsations of love. By holding awareness in your heart, you have access to the highest states.

Notice any quality shifts—perhaps a clear state, feeling more composed, calm, or an experience of homecoming. Your physical, mental, and emotional states might feel more balanced. Relax into whatever state or experience emerges. Be in it. You are paying a visit to the temple. You can return here regularly.

To increase our capacity to reside in regenerative emotions and attitudes, a powerful choice is to visit our heart's temple often. As we honor and repeatedly soak in the power and wisdom of our divine heart, we benefit from the temple's luminosity. Ardently engaging with our heart, we will embrace our sublime destiny of love, light, and joy.

Inhabiting the sacred temple, our heart communicates thankfulness, happiness, serenity. Our whole being tingles with delight. As we appreciate and sustain the heart's resonance, our awareness increases, and positive emotions prevail. We can bask in the warmth of their wonderment. We can honor each emergence by often recalling and savoring the experience.

REMEMBRANCE IS A POTENT CATALYST

Each time we remember, we amplify and anchor within our psyche the vibratory force of an experience. The fastening that takes place in remembrance reshapes our energy and raises our heart's capacity to absorb more love, light, and joy. With heightened resonance, strength adds to our journey. Over time, encounters with these blissful occasions multiply. Each one becomes submerged within our heart-space, building a potent, vast magnetic field. This magnetism powerfully draws us toward our dream, our sacred destiny.

To support our quest, we can consciously and consistently create spaciousness during our day—space for warmheartedness, lightheartedness, breathing with our heart, serving others, being in nature, resting in stillness, offering gratitude. Fanning the flame of our heart, we travel, letting go of resistance that arises. When we encounter blocks on the way to the temple, we benefit from taking a careful look, amusing ourselves by removing each barrier, whatever its popularity, justification, or importance.

Strolling past our loneliness and forgetfulness, we can welcome other longing hearts we meet. We will recognize and be drawn to guidance that immensely helps us stride forward. As we frequent the sacred space within, our repertoire of clarity, joy, and expansiveness builds. The pathway to the temple of our heart becomes unhindered, instinctive.

The more often we step into and linger in the temple, the more dazzled by the brilliance our whole being becomes. The radiant light energizes us, fills us with bliss.

It is within our power to live here, love from here, create miracles from this abiding light and space of profound contentment. Then, due to our courage and perseverance, we know we will dwell in the place of all our yearning.

IGNITING FIRES

Pure Love throbs inside your precious heart
craving to be expressed
like wild horses running free.

Its flames lavish warmth, tenderness.
Light, resplendent light
unleashes fervor—
destroying fear and isolation.

Every word, touch, look rekindles embers.
Luminous hearts blaze,
setting the world aglow.

CHAPTER 2
Are We Aware?

We are busy, busy bees, driven through our days by thoughts of what to do, how to act, what we desire and deserve to have, how we need to prove ourselves, how we prioritize what is essential, and the list continues. In that speedy chaos, we miss the wisdom our heart has to offer. When our heart asks us to pause, step outdoors, smile at another person, relax at lunch, honor a commitment, listen to the breeze, pardon ourselves or another, or simply rest, we instead maintain a frenzied stride, moving forward.

It is understandable that while zillions of thoughts fly through our mind at the speed of light, we can be distracted from the profound mystery of our heart. How compelling thoughts are. It can feel dizzying to keep track of them. Our mind, filled to the brim, works like a robust tugboat maneuvering hulking input throughout the day.

Whether positive or negative, no matter what the topic, our thoughts produce different states within us. It is good to remember that our state impacts our heart, our attitudes, and our interactions. Have you thought about how your thoughts impact you, your heart, your life?

Personally and professionally, many of us have become unconscious, automatic, and habitual about the way we think, see, and process what is before us. Reflect on your life: Have you ever arrived home after a long day and realized you had no memory of the commute?

Was that commute taken in a daze?

Where was your mind? Were you connected to your heart?

Over time, as we ignore our heart's whispers, we become numb to the present moment, the signals around us, and our heart's invitations. This comatose-like state has us walking around in a daze, feeling lonely and lost, not involved in events or enjoying the people in our lives.

When we are unsure about what we have been thinking, our emotions can be significant clues to uncover our mind's play. We can check our feeling state by merely tuning in to ourselves: Notice, how do you feel? When we get in touch with our emotional state, we can backtrack to see what was occurring in our mind. We'll be able to see the inner dialogue. Also, if there is a litany of negative emotions, we can assume that our thoughts will not serve our heart's highest desires.

TRIUMPH

The heart whispers to us often throughout each day, helping us to stay balanced and joyful. It recognizes when we have distanced ourselves from it and calls us gently back to bathe in its grace. It reminds us to pause, breathe, relax, let go, connect in the moment. We need to get good at listening to our heart and not set aside its invitations. The more we listen and follow its whispers, the more clarity develops and happiness follows.

It is a practice. It takes becoming quiet enough to be conscious of what is transpiring inside. We might currently have layers of thoughts of who we believe ourselves to be. Whether seasoned with self-doubt or self-importance, their effect is essentially the same: They distort reality. They hold us back from living graciously. We can't hear or see correctly, and we don't know it.

We need to develop more acute awareness—getting good at noticing our inner topography. Awareness is quiet and untroubled, like leisurely reclining next to a lazy river on a vacation day, conscious of the ripples as they bubble past. It is a subtle, silent noticing.

When we focus on the present moment—the textures, colors, and scents that are in our current environment—we become more aware. Our breath automatically relaxes; we shift into our body. We become present in our heart. Then we can look at the screen of our mind to take note of what is transpiring.

We benefit when we expand our vision to see what has been heretofore unseen. It takes an inward gaze of the heart that looks beyond the familiar terrain. Our thoughts are an excellent entryway into being more attentive. We can ask: Are these thoughts uplifting my spirit? What might my heart want me to see, to hear?

Awareness needs to develop. For me, that means turn down the volume of the world, undo some of my habitual patterns, look with childlike curiosity at myself. No judgment; just noticing, witnessing. It takes a willingness to become quiet, with an open and available heart. It is a gentle, kindhearted observation.

Pause for a second and imagine walking down a street. In addition to seeing nature, we notice someone in a top hat, someone carrying an umbrella, someone riding a bike, a couple holding hands, a car speeding past, an ice cream cone on the pavement. Are we able to see without busying our mind, without opinions? It takes time and willingness to develop this refinement. Once we do, we are not bound by our stories. Instead, we are free to see, hear, love.

HELPFUL HINTS FOR DEEPENING AWARENESS

Choose one suggestion from the following list and use it as a practice each day. It will open many avenues to see and appreciate so much more.

- Spend quality time connecting inwardly with music.
- Name the cloud images you see gliding across the sky.

- Find moments throughout the day to simply be still.
- Listen with genuine appreciation to others' viewpoints.
- Cultivate in yourself one special quality you admire in others.
- Walk from your car to your destination simply being aware, noticing.
- Replay an uncomfortable situation with curiosity about your contribution.
- Do something as fundamental as changing a morning routine
- Or, even a little less complicated, change the order of putting on shoes or buttoning a top.

Each activity can open an avenue to heightened perception. We interrupt a routine and allow ourselves to be more present and in the moment. Once we build the capacity of being present, our awareness starts to flow into other aspects of our day. Through taking time and devoting practice, competency develops.

"I'm too busy," that little voice in your head may be saying. "These sound like great ideas for people who aren't so busy." Well, look again. The suggestions take willingness, not time. They require only an intention and a shift of awareness from our usual routine. Though small, they can make a huge difference in our lives.

Every moment abounds with vibrant energy. When we hold fast to the heart's quality of connection, we create extraordinary experiences. No matter the roles we play, following our heart's rhythm can make a difference of night and day. Our heart's pulsations guide us to an ever-expanded understanding. We begin to embrace our inestimable good fortune of being here, in relation to other people and the world around us.

Paying attention to our heart's whispers establishes within us a pathway to wisdom, to serenity, to being a warmhearted human.

Every time we revisit our inner awareness, it offers us the comfort of returning home. Clarity occurs, providing solutions and warding off accidents and illness. Awareness reduces tension and initiates more trusting and profound bonds with others. Awareness generates a life of joy.

MASTER CLOCK

Imagine a Master Clock nonchalantly ticking
one predictable second after another
unfurling time to generate life's stories.

Like the click, click, click of the train on its tracks,
you are well on your way.
How does your passport read?

Did you plan, choose,
take the route that will get you to your desired destination?
Are you too busy? Did you allow enough time?

Possibly without agreement, you are already traveling in time.
Listen to quiet awareness pulsing in your heart.
Respect its prompts.

Boldly launch your exceptional adventure—
perfect and timely expression
yours, truly yours.
Rejoice!

CHAPTER 3
Our Breath

Who is the friend who continually remains at our side throughout our entire life? Who is the one we often disregard? Our most wondrous and essential, life-giving breath is our perpetual friend. By deepening our relationship with this companion, we become the recipient of all it has to offer, in moments of joy as well as stress. We can turn to this faithful friend for support. In our breath, everything becomes possible. As we embrace our life force's power and benefits, we will be vastly happier, more content, and at peace—guaranteed 100 percent.

The breath is continually serving our moment-to-moment needs. A car next to us slams on its brakes, and we hold our breath for a moment until we regain composure. We run a marathon or perform some extraordinary physical exertion, and we might gasp for breath. We laugh with delight until our belly aches. We sleep peacefully, faintly inhaling and exhaling, soft as the gentlest murmur of breath in a sleeping infant. The breath is a steady, reliable friend. No matter what is happening in a day, the breath continues to come and go. We might feel scared or happy, upstaged or honored, guilty or innocent—our life force always serves, is on call and in movement.

There are multiple ways language references this dear companion of ours: I need to save my breath; it takes my breath away; a breath of fresh air; with bated breath; catch my breath; out of breath; take a deep breath; in the same breath; don't hold your breath; with every breath; don't waste your breath; and more. All these phrases, packed with meaning, generate distinct energy, thoughts, and emotions.

I FORGET

If you are anything like me, you may have taken your breath for granted. Interestingly, you may have noticed it more acutely when you held your breath, when you felt tense, afraid to take a step or move forward. Internal clutching is caused by feeling you are not enough or believing that you cannot do whatever is needed.

I have also experienced needing a deep breath just to get started, to get myself out of being stalled and in motion again.

Breathing is natural, a universal process that all of us share. The energy in our bodies is in constant motion. The movement is quite evident when watching a sleeping baby or the faithful repetitions of our inhalations and exhalations. However, the breath can offer us much more than its familiar, comforting tempo.

Fortunately, over the years, I have been blessed to study with masters of breath. They taught me ancient wisdom about the science and philosophy of this ever-nourishing gift. It is our ultimate healer, our wise teacher. Our breath instructs and maintains everything in our being.

Our breath can rescue us from unwanted thoughts and emotions and improve the way we interact with others. Its influence in our lives can be profound, especially when we consciously embrace the breath as an ever-present companion.

OUR BREATH IS A REGULATOR

A natural, relaxed breathing pace can be profoundly healing and revitalizing to our whole being. Think of the breath as the conductor of the phenomenal symphony of our mind, body, and spirit. Following this inspired conductor's lead enriches our lives and offers us countless gifts. When our breath is in a state of equilibrium, we experience contentment; our vision is open and unhindered; we make clear decisions. We engage with people in sincere, benevolent, and honest ways.

The opposite is true when we are tense, absorbed with unsettling thoughts. When we are anxious or upset, our energy is disrupted and out of sorts. As our mind and body become constrained, our breathing becomes shallow and perhaps rapid. Our heart might even feel compressed. We feel stuck in these predicaments. Our whole system slips into a contracted state, which causes us to react curtly rather than respond graciously.

By consciously yielding to a slower, longer breathing rhythm, we disperse negative charges. We change our energetic frequency by consciously exhaling smoothly, allowing the next inhalation to arise naturally. As we release and receive each breath gently, dissatisfaction and disappointment fade. Our inhalations and exhalations become more even and smooth. The breath balances and many subtle levels of agitation dissipate.

This cooperation with our breath is a soft, silky, receptive act. It is as natural as laughter arising from playing peekaboo with a baby; we don't need to exert effort. Relax into it; receive it. We need not judge or rush to change the breath. Instead, we can trust the breath as we would a dear friend. When honored, it will connect us wholly to ourselves.

Our breath is dynamic and responsive. Our breath is the liberator. Our all-wise friend oversees each situation and responds effectively.

EQUANIMITY

Imagine Conscious Power always in balance—
never disturbing an internal state.
Like a bareback rider easily reseating when slipping,
claim unruffled steadiness—
absorbing all with sunny composure.

Sense this freer place slightly below the surface of thoughts—
serene, peaceful, unaffected,
pure energy in motion.
Relaxed, deep, even breaths brighten the pathway.

Dip beneath the exterior world,
enter your heart,
welcome clear vision, strength, discernment.
Embody calm equanimity
one conscious breath at a time.

CHAPTER 4

Engage with Your Dearest Friend

Even now, you can bring a soft focus to your breath as you experience these suggestions.

Allow a gentle awareness to follow the sensation of cooling air as it enters your nostrils and travels inside. Notice where it comes to rest until it is ready to depart. Feel its warmth as it calmly leaves.

Relax into an unhurried tempo. Thoughtfully repeat this sequence several times, noticing the breath's natural destination in the heart.

Observe the fluid flow of your breathing. See how a mindful shift in awareness already alters the breath.

Become conscious of your breath's cadence and intentionally partner with it. Just as you would take someone's hand to help you climb a steep slope, allow the breath to guide you.

Release and receive its movement effortlessly. Your loving attention to your friend is reciprocal and multiplied. Breathing consciously, allow stress to recede more and more on the exhalations. Notice a gentle expansion and releasing in your torso with each leisurely repetition.

Grow in wonder and appreciation for every inhalation and exhalation. Discover how outer circumstances and needing to control things begin to fade. Notice the breath's calming effect. Your whole being receives a clean slate, an opportunity to breathe fully and comfortably as you experience a more fluid flow of conscious energy moving through you.

Take all the time you need for the next exhalation—no need to hurry.

Continue with a steady, calm cadence, experiencing the pauses between breaths.

Sense how fresh, revitalized energy begins to soothe you.

Listen and hear your breath's pleasing resonance.

Give yourself space to experience each new awareness that arises, in the same way that there is space between these lines, space between inhalations and exhalations.

Your muscles relax as additional barriers to freedom dissolve and drop away.

With more leisurely repetitions, allow thoughts and emotions to evaporate.

Notice the incoming and outgoing breaths becoming smooth, equal, and balanced.

Your nervous system responds by relaxing. Your whole being is imbued with serenity.

One by one, each in-breath and out-breath deepens peace, contentment, and kindheartedness. Your mind becomes still and tranquil. Entering heaven on earth, consent to rest here, in this delightful comfort, for a little while longer.

MERGING KNOWLEDGE, EXPERIENCE, PRACTICE

The power of our breath is with us in each moment. We don't have to run back home to get it, nor do we need cash in our pocket. The breath is ours, and its untapped power is enormous. When we slip into its natural flow, our inner world opens into quietude. The breath breathes us into wholeness. We live more in harmony.

All that isn't needed dissolves away like snow melting on a sun-drenched day; we return to our true self, settled in our heart. The earth herself rejoices and welcomes us wholeheartedly.

Our mind, heart, and body's symphony is exquisite. We have more access to creativity, wisdom, vitality, connection to others, joy, strength, and contentment. We can relate to circumstances and others with clarity, sensitivity, and generosity. Now, more resilient, we are ready to pursue our destiny consciously and joyously.

Our breath can give us immense help simply because we embrace its presence. Sometimes we are confused, scared, in physical pain, at odds with another person, about to face a difficult situation, or worried. We don't need to multiply the tension that those pressures create. We don't need to hold our breath or allow fear and apprehension to create a breath pattern that undermines us further.

Instead, once we become aware, we join our breath and ride it to freedom. Begin with noticing.

Then practice these simple steps:

1. Acknowledge your breath.
    a. Mindfully follow it as it enters.
    b. Release it gently and unhurriedly.
    c. Allow the muscles in your face, shoulders, and body to release and let go.
2. Become inwardly malleable and receptive.
    a. Yield to the breath's rhythm.
    b. Allow your inhalations and exhalations to become smooth, equal, and balanced.
    c. Glide into a serene, inner space with ease.
3. Choose how to act benevolently from this clearer, revitalized state.

As our appreciation for our breath increases and our relationship with it deepens, we will be able to stay more consistently calm, centered, and steadfast. We can practice connecting with our breath everywhere— at home, in the office, at a park, before we fall asleep, when we awake. The more often we consciously practice, the deeper our connection to the breath as the gateway to inner and outer freedom.

Then, in moments of need, we can naturally glide into this more balanced state. Our relationships can thrive because we are authentic, established in the present, receptive, and approachable. By allowing ourselves to become less tense and stressed, we have become more.

One of the masters I've learned with is Mary Burmeister. She would say to me, "Every breath, well-lived, makes yesterday a dream of happiness and tomorrow ecstasy."

Enjoy your breath and the freedom it offers.

CHAPTER 5
The Bright Path Forward

Did you know that science speaks about recognition as the ability of molecules with complementary shapes to attach to one another? I find that fascinating. The study of the physical and natural world is eye-opening. Science is continually revealing the creation of unimaginable wonder. Each discovery adds a gem to a vibrant string of jewels. Through ongoing examination and research, each breakthrough increases our understanding and appreciation of this marvelous world. Previous beliefs that seemed like absolute truth undergo revision.

And yet, in our typical, everyday life, it is easy for us to believe only what we can see, what we can understand, and what fits into the certainties of life as we know life to be. Whatever we already value and experience seem totally real to us, as if they were "the complete truth." We get glimpses that there is so much more to experience. At the same time, our carefully trained radar keeps searching out that which is comfortable and validates our usual way of thinking and seeing.

Even as our knowledge bank increases and expands, we define the limits of what we are willing to understand or what we believe is possible. What our "reality" is can either remain quite the same or be modified again and again. In concert with and with respect for scientific knowledge, ancient cultures often honor additional ways of knowing, seeing, and interacting with the world. I was fortunate to be included on paths of ancient wisdom that opened my eyes to possibilities that I may not otherwise have seen or entertained.

WORKING WITH A MEDICINE MAN STRETCHED MY PERCEPTION

In the mid-1980s, a new way of seeing rocked my world. For four years, I studied with an Aztec Indian medicine man named Mike Valenzuela. He was a free and happy-spirited man, with remarkable gifts and a generous heart. He was content, self-assured, and easygoing; I seldom saw a hint of annoyance, which was an entirely different experience from the attitudes I grew up around. At first, he felt a little unreal to me.

Studying at his side continually scrambled and rearranged my brain. My entire apprenticeship with him was one of learning to see and recognize what was invisible to the eyes. I struggled to understand the seemingly un-understandable.

Mike received his ability from his grandfather, and he wished to pass on what he had learned. He introduced me to a vision of subtleties. It was a life beyond what our eyes observe in everyday experience. It arose from being established in the experience of the heart. Time and time again, Mike urged me to put down fear, doubt, and resistance to enter this immutable realm. His powerful guidance would become a lifelong endeavor.

Mike's grandfather taught him a unique healing and balanced way. From age three until age eighteen, he lived with and trained with his father's father, a well-known medicine man in Guatemala. As an adult, Mike spoke about how clear his mind was at that young age and how easy it was to receive this outstanding education and power. For example, he learned anatomy by watching his grandfather draw the different body systems in the sand. Mike said he would observe the sand come to life; he could see the organs move and the sand-body's energy flowing. This is just one anecdote, Mike shared. There were many such examples he told during my years of study with him.

When I apprenticed with Mike, he was helping Native Americans from many different tribes in the western United States. He could determine the source of people's illnesses and restore their body, mind, spirit, and emotions to wellness. How could this medicine man see that the source of someone's illness was deep-seated sorrow from the loss of a cherished friend? How could a woman who had not walked for many years leave the treatment room walking independently? How did tumors melt away? How did he know that anger or hatred was lurking in someone's heart? I saw these and many other ailments and injuries successfully resolved.

In temporary rooms set up on austere reservation sites, literally hundreds of people would come and stand in line for healing. I particularly remember a sun-wrinkled man on a piercingly cold winter day. He stood in line all morning waiting his turn to ask the question, "How much?" Given the answer of twenty dollars, he walked and hitchhiked more than an hour to the nearest city to pawn his turquoise jewelry for the twenty dollars he needed. When the man came back, he stood in line again, waiting his turn. Although I mention this one individual, this was not a unique story of the trust people had in Mike. I witnessed a multitude of similar expressions of confidence and conviction.

People came to Mike because this medicine man was authentic. He could cure their suffering. He knew how to be truly present in each moment with every person—seeing their beauty and pain. He relaxed in silence, believing that everything they needed was already there, present in the moment.

His seeing and knowing weren't a consequence of the stories people told him, because he often didn't understand their language. Mike told me that his knowledge came from a subtle inner vision. I could feel that was true. Mike dedicated his life to seeing the seemingly invisible and wanted to pass his ability on to others. The powerful medicine he offered was in seeing each person from his heart; he sincerely cared. His inner vision was pristine. He knew how to allow his heart to merge with each person and bring understanding and resolution to light.

In contrast to Mike's life, our way of perceiving the world might seem a bit limited or ordinary. I share this snapshot with you to throw open possibilities of moments that are perhaps beyond your present experience and understanding, let alone believable. They might excite your mind to embrace glimpses of what many have not seen, and yet what exists.

In both practical and spiritual ways, the years of witnessing disease and its resolution under Mike's care opened my vision. To join Mike in his world, I needed to become free of control, opinion, and judgment. For me, Mike's concept that everything that the person needed was already available continues to swirl through my mind. It unfolds in my heart, even now, long after I worked with him.

MORE THAN EYE CAN SEE

Since the turn of the century, a parallel theme has caught my attention. I am studying a commentary on an ancient Kashmir Shaivism text, pondering the concept that every particle in the universe contains the fundamental nature of creation. This view can be explained by thinking about each seed carrying a map of instructions for all to come. We'll broaden our scope of vision by exploring just one seed's expression through many aspects.

By way of illustration, let's reflect on the mighty banyan tree.

- Its seed is hard and small, already containing everything it needs to grow—the whole of its creation.
- It is not unusual for the banyan tree to reach one hundred feet in height and cover several acres of ground.

- When one of its seeds drops on a leaf and germinates, its innate intelligence sends down roots into the ground; this new tree becomes part of its host and might even become another trunk.
- The tree's continuous relationship with the sun, the earth, the air, and other elements allows it to thrive throughout a couple of hundred years. Each stage of its evolution contains the whole.

Our understanding can penetrate deeper yet; we can appreciate the following:

- The banyan tree is a living being replete with stories and moments of history it has embraced, as it offered and still offers a shaded canopy to villagers and travelers.
- We could say that the banyan tree is generous. The tree is native to India, and in Hindi, its name translates as the "wish-fulfilling tree." Its life force, ever in motion, pulses through pores and veins, creating healing properties within every part of its design.
- Roots, seeds, fruit, sap, leaves, and bark are all beneficial for health. From toothaches to infertility to ulcers, the illnesses that these bountiful trees cure are many.
- Villagers feel a bond with the tree and act with respect and gratitude toward it.
- Indian myths and tales venerate the tree as sacred. People believe it embodies the Lord Himself as creator, sustainer, and the one who reabsorbs all phenomena.
- The tree's vast umbrella creates a spiritual retreat, an oasis of inner stillness and tranquility. Its expansive canopy lends itself to being a place of refuge, a holy place that welcomes everyone.

I have been fortunate to sit beneath the banyan tree's umbrella in India and on Kauai, one of the Hawaiian Islands. Each time, I have felt its comforting, abiding presence penetrating and soothing my weariness and fear—opening my mind and heart to warmth, love, and peace.

There is considerably more in a seed or moment in time than a cursory view can convey. How open are we to discovering what is invisible? What will we discover when seeing with our heart?

For years, I witnessed incredible healings while Mike worked. I walked with women healers whom I will never forget and to whom I will always be grateful. They are my sisters who continue to walk with me.

I experienced hidden wisdom and sacredness on reservations in America and on the hallowed grounds of India. I am deeply grateful for all these blessed opportunities. Such a bright path I was able to travel. It opened my mind to wonder. It fed my heart and soul and enriched my life tremendously.

CHAPTER 6
Intrinsic Sacredness

In many indigenous cultures, people feel in communion with the natural world. They believe that the physical world issues from and encompasses a divine presence as real as the material world—the spiritual and material are inseparable worlds. Just as wetness is a feature of water and warmth is inherent in the sun.

I've heard it told that in the Solomon Islands, when the natives want a part of the forest for their civilization, they don't cut down trees. They simply gather around a tree and shout abuses to their hearts' content. They curse it.

In a matter of days, the tree withers and shrivels. It dies on its own.

Native peoples appreciate, value, and embrace an intrinsic partnership with all things. Texts of the ancient East explain how this spiritual world exists as the purest vibration of energy, which is often referred to with different names. In China, this energy is called ch'i or qi; in India, it is prana; and in Japan, it is ki. Each Native American tribe also addresses this energy by name.

This pure energy organizes and reshapes itself into myriad forms while retaining its essential nature. It is the source from which our expansive skies, great blue oceans, radiant stars, verdant plant life, and wild things of various dimensions and sizes come into being. It permeates all living things and creates us as humans with thoughts, dreams, physical sensations, power, and experiences. This energy is often called the light that exists throughout and within everything in this colorful universe.

No matter how distant we feel from our experience as light, our inner being is unspoiled. At the core of each of us as humans is that pure essence interacting with the selfsame energy in all we encounter. When we release into this truth, we expand into more. We access other ways of seeing and knowing.

Bathed in the serenity of our precious heart, we stretch into this understanding and experience that profundity. As our relationship with our heart deepens, our mind expands. We are freed from fear and disabling emotions, becoming more present. It takes an inward gaze to look beyond our familiar terrain of comparisons and judgments. With courage and care, we can step into the sphere of the unknown ready to be surprised, ready to be reshaped.

Benevolence escorts us over a threshold of limitation into a place where great wisdom, power, and joy reside. In this way, we can access a vast, elevated state of being. And as we enter this realm, we arrive, stunned, at the place where everything that is needed is already there.

We are like the banyan seed. The seeds within the tree and within us can grow in time into magnificence. We are like each particle in the universe described by Kashmir Shaivism. Each of us has all we need to fulfill our greatest potential, to grace the lives of those we encounter, to leave this world a better place. To access this power, we must open to it, believe, and act in a way that supports this truth: all we require already exists within us.

This way of thinking might sound audacious, esoteric, and mystical. However, expanding into a subtle perspective like this can benefit us in daily life and manifest in ways beyond understanding.

Ancient cultures have appreciated this mystery, and science is discovering it is so.

> After many years on dialysis, my daughter Anita's kidney function was failing at an escalating rate. Even increasing the number or length of treatments wasn't helping. Her energy was depleted, her spirits low. At times, she felt hopeless, trapped.
>
> She had been on a transplant list, courageously waiting. However, on many trips to the Mayo Clinic, with meticulous intake and prep all completed, the doctor would come into the room. He would apologize, saying that the kidney would not be a fit for her. Of course, she was disappointed each time.
>
> Through all the challenges, her heart continued to radiate love and compassion for others. Deep inside, her heart knew and Anita trusted that the perfect match would come.
>
> Then, one Saturday, while receiving her fourth dialysis treatment of the week, the Mayo Clinic called saying she should promptly get to the clinic. Her brother picked her up. When they arrived at the clinic, the doctors were at the door to greet her. The kidney, her kidney waiting for her, was a complete match.
>
> What miracles!!! As of this writing, we've had the privilege of enjoying Anita's humor, wisdom, and love for four more years.

As we recognize the greatness that lives in us, we see it in every person. We notice precious opportunities available, even in difficulties. We feel safer, free from harm, more flexible, less irritated or anxious, more supported, and interconnected with all that is.

Our mind and heart are in alignment. We develop greater understanding, compassion, and generosity. Our perception of life and others expands. We are kinder. We don't hide or run away from pain or nuisances. Instead, courage grows and leads us forward. Contentment and joy are our companions. With more clarity, we easily solve problems that arise. We attract goodwill and love in the same way that flowers attract bees and honey draws bears.

HOW DO WE GET THERE?

We make the journey by slowing down and becoming aware, more present, in each situation. We become receptive, able to pause and cherish small moments. Our breath is welcome, easeful. We experience serene spaces between our inhalations and exhalations as we relax further, traveling deeper inside to stillness. Contentment begins to blossom.

Additionally, we can choose any of the following ways to become more steadily heart-centered:

- enjoy nature
- drink in beauty
- listen genuinely
- respect others' deepest desires
- become more "we" motivated
- honor the invitations our heart offers
- pause throughout the day to experience gratefulness
- consider situations wholeheartedly and with honesty
- embrace moments of joy and allow them to expand
- release all that weighs us down

Any one of these practices, done consistently, helps us step into subtle realms of great possibility. Our vision softens. Our heart expands and becomes more available and engaged. The mind comes to rest in the heart. Then, joined as steadfast partners, the heart and mind shine as one lustrous light. We acquire the capacity to shift our awareness and maintain equilibrium. We can meet another person genuinely—one-to-one, heart-to-heart.

To experience someone that generously open with us, having no judgment or barriers, is utterly delicious. We have no choice but to fall, tumbling head over heels, into their safe, welcoming heart—complementary shapes attaching to one another.

When we fasten all of who we are to our heart, we birth a haven that invites another person in. When someone responds warmheartedly to us, we feel it. And as we open fully to recognize and receive their essence, we create a harmonious, interrelated universe that contains everything and extends beyond the space between us. We become the bearers and receivers of love, healing, and hope. Both of us are more of our true selves, with increased capacities and energy. Together, we enter sacredness.

Although this is unfamiliar ground at first, it is what our heart longs to experience. As we become securely seated in our heart, inner strength, resolve, and wisdom support us to act gracefully. We respond and do the right thing, in the right way, at the right time. It is not a "right way" based on external rules and judgments; instead, a natural impulse emerges in the moment. The "right way" arises from our inner connection to freedom and fluidity as we serve the moment with complete presence.

Living in this way, we valiantly spread a canopy of honesty, respect, trust, and love. We are the safest when we open our heart and offer safety to others. We see the universe accurately, not filtered through any of our biases. No matter what is happening, we know how to respond because we are present, alive to this fantastic adventure called life. That is why we offer the best of ourselves, our heart.

Anita was taking a walk on a shivery, crisp predawn morning. Coming toward her was a woman inadequately dressed, shuffling slowly and pulling a small cart filled with the totality of her possessions. Turning toward the woman, Anita asked if she was cold. "Yes," was the soft whimper. Anita wrapped her

*warm scarf around the woman. This story touched my heart;
here is my response:*

*Imagine Grace afoot winding through roadways and lanes,
recognizing, appreciating simple needs.*

*Like draping gleeful arms round dearest friends,
stay connected to tenderness, affection—
wrapping those cold in warmth,
loving those whose eyes
convey fear, loneliness, hopelessness.*

*Pause often, appreciate others' dignity.
Feeding hearts with sunlit smiles
reveals heaven on earth—
Grace's hands comforting bodies and souls.*

I invite you to experience all the sacredness and delight your wondrous heart has to offer. I encourage you to be unwavering in purpose, embrace surprises, and continually challenge yourself to be receptive to what has been invisible in your world. Notice what you might be taking for granted or where you might be holding back.

What previously unseen world is opening before you? What will you see when listening with your heart? How could your influence stretch? Could it perhaps be as far-reaching and magnificent as a banyan tree or, even yet, the expansive skies?

CHAPTER 7
Who Do I See in the Mirror?

We easily determine and experience the temperature outdoors. We can feel if it is cold, warm, or hot. However, are we aware of the degree of warmth, humility, and kinship in our own heart?

I sat there in awe as the old monk answered our questions. Though I'm usually shy, I felt so comfortable in his presence that I found myself raising my hand. "Father, could you tell us something about yourself?"

He leaned back. "Myself?" he mused. There was a long pause.
"My name . . .
used to be . . .
me.
But now . . .
it's you."

from *Tales of a Magic Monastery*

Luckily, there is a great gauge we can use to measure the warmth in our heart. That gauge exists in the mirror we see in people's eyes and faces in our day-to-day life. Grace exists in each "you."

We have a concept of who we are, yet the mirrors reflect a vision of us that we might not be aware of or know. Sometimes the mirrors light up our heart with joy or giddiness, sometimes with wonder, connection, or admiration.

Those are the mirrors we love to gaze into and see ourselves. We love the reflection. We feel seen, comforted, and accepted.

However, there are challenging mirrors that are easier for us to reject or run past, pretending they do not exist. They are the ones that are difficult to glance into for more than a second or two. Those reflections cloak us with uncomfortable feelings—perhaps disbelief, anger, hurt, shame, guilt, or insignificance. No wonder it is painful to look—our self-image feels challenged and bruised.

There are two reasons for this. First, unknowingly, we are seduced by who we believe ourselves to be, and second, we feel separate from others and the mirror they reflect. It is easy to convince ourselves that the mirror (which the other reflects to us) is distorted or inaccurate. In those circumstances, we probably work hard to change the mirror or clutch onto a belief that the reflection is wrong. We simply cannot take in what we see in the mirror. We sprint away.

A new client, Jean-Luc, felt upset and unsettled. His discontent was affecting his work. Married thirty-odd years, he was sure the faults his wife observed in him were not valid.

After speaking together for a short while, I could feel his good heart. I asked him to go back in his mind to the time they met. I wanted to hear every detail that was fascinating about the woman he met and how he fell in love with her.

Jean-Luc dropped denial and opened his heart. You could feel sparks bursting into flames. His heart was ready to see what his wife saw. Jean-Luc's memories connected him to all he desired and had committed to in his marriage.

Their rekindled love is burning brightly years later. Together, the family found what they had lost.

WE BENEFIT FROM DARING TO LOOK AT WHAT WE'VE RUN FROM.

Whether our self-image is one of self-doubt or self-importance, the effect is essentially the same. Our vision is compromised. The rigidity of our self-opinion causes our pain and suffering. More importantly, the certainty of our conviction traps us into feeling separate from others and lonely. It does not allow us to discover truth and move toward happiness. We sense the disconnect, but we are caught in a struggle to maintain our view and hold tighter to the image that needs to shift. We need to make room for more information.

Here is a perfect time to slow down rather than speed up past a mirror. We need to believe in our life's accumulated resources and muster up all the stamina it takes to pause and look. Right across from us, in the mirror, is our path to a happier life. We need to make room in our heart to receive this gift. Yes, it takes courage.

This kind of courage feels like standing at the top of the Grand Canyon with your toes hanging over the edge. With that much grit and resolve, we need to let go, open, and step forward to see what others see. Buoyed up, we become curious and willing to be reshaped. It is a magical moment and a vulnerable place that requires humility. We can take refuge in knowing these truths:

- Nothing reflected can harm us.
- The present mirror is salient and ideally placed to peel back all that is not true and does not serve our highest self.
- Grace accompanies the reflection; we are ready to see.
- Our capacity for joy increases in direct proportion to our willingness to explore our discomfort.
- The effort to see with a pure heart gives us the life we long to live.

As we are looking into these mirrors, the moments of difficulty we feel exist as invitations to adjust our vision. They remind us to pause, breathe, relax, and let go into a new, more all-embracing story we can have of ourselves. The more we relax and do not resist what another person's eyes and expressions mirror, the freer and happier we will become.

> Imagine the Most Radiant One making visible
> wonder, beauty—
> your pristine heart, the source of all that is good.
>
> Like early morning's unblemished snow-blanket,
> affirm your virtue—I am an
> unspoiled, perfect, beautiful, fully beloved being.
>
> Embrace this reflection of yourself, drink it in
> way down to your toes
> till they wiggle with delight.
>
> Peel back any remaining notions that are not light, bright you.
> Believe—I am an
> unspoiled, perfect, beautiful, fully beloved being.

This poem speaks the truth. Allow yourself to relax into feeling deeply loved and accepted. Once you appreciate that you are beautiful and perfect, mirrors will not frighten you. They will appear, and you will be able to meet them with calm, honest aplomb. You will see yourself in the other and the other in you—no more two. If ever, or whenever, you need a helping hand, ponder these questions.

Ask:

How might I remember to pause? . . . to step into courageous
self-exploration?

What could be possible if I allow fear to dissolve?

What benefits might come from being curious?

Will I allow myself to be happier and freer by daring to see?

CHAPTER 8
What Did Henny-Penny Need?

During any crisis (small or large), we may feel anxious. However, our mind can be a marvelous asset. It can help us navigate uncertainty. Ancient sages and modern science encourage us to understand that our mind is an incredible creative force.

We see how the mind can help progress the evolution of humanity. The mind can solve seemingly intractable problems. We witness a global family pull together in times of crisis.

The mind imagines and creates harmony and beauty. It inspires greatness and moments of insight. With the help of the heart, the mind generates love. It influences our state of being.

How remarkable life would be if we consistently reaped our mind's benefits. Since a calm, resourceful mind is always possible, why don't we have a steadier experience of its vast capacity? Why do we experience so many limitations? We'll look at our mind together to find out why.

THE SKY IS FALLING

I know what it is like to experience my mind wandering carelessly—to hear its incessant chatter, to feel captivated by its juicy web of stories. I know what it is like to be its fear-filled hostage, feeling as though the thoughts running through my mind have power over me.

Dilemmas like these remind me of a fairy tale I heard as a child. It was the Old English version of the Chicken Little story, called "Henny-Penny." It contains bits of silliness and fear and provides a great metaphor for the experience of our mind. The story begins like this:

> One day Henny-Penny was picking up corn in the corn-yard when whack!—something hit her upon the head. "Goodness, gracious me!" cried Henny-Penny. "The sky's a-going to fall; I must go and tell the king."

Her response to her thoughts sent her on a dutiful mission. Henny-Penny fearfully scurries along, gathering several of her feathered friends. She convinces each of them that the sky is falling. She needs them to join her as allies to add credibility to her story as she tells the king.

Even though Henny-Penny's fear is unfounded, the tale clearly demonstrates how the mind works. Perhaps we can learn from her and use our challenging moments as opportunities to make a leap in understanding and create peace of mind.

CREATING A WORLD

Wherever we focus our mind, we create reality. Henny-Penny and her friends focused on this dreadful catastrophe that they believed was happening. These silly birds are like all the energy we pour into the thoughts that seize our attention. We, humans, not only create a world through our thoughts, we sustain what we create. Once thoughts drive our perspective, we move like puppets, reacting to whatever strings our thoughts pull.

Our mind, a little like Henny-Penny's, can have us scurry through corn-yards, building proof and intensity about our version of whatever story is alive for us. The fairy tale goes on to tell us that the lot of these barnyard friends fall prey to the cunning of Foxey-Loxey.

The feathered friends are so obsessed with the sky falling that they abandon their usual wariness of foxes.

Sometimes in our lives, it might feel like everything is a crisis, maybe even out to get us. However, we are more fortunate than Henny-Penny, because we have a great mind.

If the sages and science are correct, our mind can create much more than disparaging opinions or disastrous scenarios.

Here's a key question: In a distressing time, how can we help our mind lead us in a positive direction and make healthy decisions that support us?

What if we made our mind our friend? I believe that's the answer! Let's create a relationship with our mind as a friend, as a companion who can help us experience quiet, calm, beauty, and contentment. To do that, we will need to get to know it a little better.

ESTABLISH A GOOD RELATIONSHIP

We own this valuable real estate. We know it as our mind. *Pure*, *perfect*, and *phenomenal* are its most elevated attributes. The mind's capacity to experience bliss and love far surpasses our usual experience. We discover the mind's depths only when we allow it to rest in stillness beyond all thoughts and desires.

Our mind and our thoughts are intimately related, not two separate objects. The mind is energy that takes the form of thoughts. Our mind is in a constant state of receptivity and formation.

The mind-play that takes place is like watching a magician juggling a multitude of assorted items. We become spellbound. We choose which item or items to notice.

Similarly, thoughts are always moving through our mind. Like the juggled items, we choose which one or ones to concentrate on and embellish. Those choices, along with the elaborations and feelings we add to them, create mental outlooks, attitudes, and demeanors.

The mind thinks almost as if it is continually searching for its unfettered state—to recover its pure nature. It isn't our task to stop thinking; that is nearly impossible. What we can do is this: become aware of our thoughts, witness them, and choose where we put our attention.

Our ability to direct thoughts happens when we become friends with our mind. Rather than allowing the mind to act like an unruly rascal that decides how to think and behave, we can pause and notice.

What is also crucial to note is that since the mind is ours, we can decide what we do with what we think. That might sound unbelievable in circumstances when it seems that our mind is the one that is in control.

OUR CHOICE

How we respond to each thought is our choice. Even though that might feel impossible at times, we have that much power. With practice, we can direct our life better. It is essential to know that we are in charge.

We create our state of mind, choice by choice. Some thoughts lead to contentment and connection to the people and events in our lives. Other thoughts drain the energy and joy right out of us, producing a drastic change of state.

Distressing and harsh thoughts constrict the mind. When the mind is continually wound tight in dark thoughts and concerns, it loses elasticity, perspective, and the capacity to see and make good decisions.

In Henny-Penny's tale, her thought of the sky falling consumed her. It seemed logical. The more she repeated it, the stronger her story became. She reinforced it with emotional energy. Now there was a worldview built around impending danger.

Henny-Penny lost perspective and became entangled and began drowning in a quagmire of fear. Her experience became limited and shackled by her mind's cleverness. Her reaction was all-consuming. As a result, Henny-Penny lost sight of choice. Her fear-filled reaction to the situation damaged her peace of mind and her "barnyard" relationships.

Yes, we are thinking beings. That is most excellent. The problem is that frequently, like Henny-Penny, we believe our thoughts are correct; we get attached to them. Then we amplify them until they take up all our mind-space. Sometimes, we end up anesthetized or inflamed by our own supersized reactions.

FREEING OURSELVES

When our mind is our friend, we spot and observe the unconstructive thoughts and resultant feelings that do not serve our happiness. As we become conscious of a crippling thought, we can pause. Merely stepping back and watching our thoughts, becoming the witness, can help us see and understand ourselves. This noticing creates space and interrupts a harmful chain reaction.

What could have happened if Henny-Penny paused? What if she had created an interval between the whack on her head and her reaction? We don't know, because Henny-Penny chose to draw a definite, immediate conclusion. A simple pause, accented with reflection, would have given her breathing space and could have changed the course of events.

Noticing, pausing, and suspending abrupt reactions allows us to see with clarity and make a more conscious choice. Pausing with awareness always serves us well, especially when thoughts are intense, obsessive, or upsetting.

In a more aware state, we can notice when we are not feeling joyful.

We have the power to choose to befriend our mind and transmute sadness and worry into contentment and quiet calm. Our mind surely is a remarkable asset.

LESSONS FROM THE BARNYARD

We have all had Henny-Penny days in our lives. Each moment is a new beginning. Our mind is incredibly malleable and amenable to change. Its capacity can expand to be steady, strong, fearless, discerning, and able to focus. It can free us, and consequently others, from suffering.

By making our mind our friend, we unlock its many great qualities. Old, conditioned patterns and reactions dissolve as we continue to cultivate rapport. We progress through life engaged in a steady and undisturbed state, with more buoyancy and confidence. Unnecessary thoughts and emotions no longer have power over us. We are less likely to be eaten by a fox.

Our mind's dialogue will remain. However, with practice, we can be in a good relationship with it.

> When the mind is at peace,
> the world too is at peace.
> Nothing real, nothing absent.
> Not holding on to reality,
> not getting stuck in the void,
> you are neither holy nor wise, just
> an ordinary fellow who has completed his work.

Layman P'ang (c. 740–808)
from *The Enlightened Heart*, 34

FORMULA FOR BEFRIENDING YOUR MIND

Make your mind your friend:

1. Pause.
   a. Notice disabling thoughts.
   b. Create space to see. Step back and witness without judgment.

2. Reflect.
    a. Consider: Are the thoughts stimulating joy and expansion or contraction?
    b. Make a conscious choice not to be attached to or amplify the thoughts.
3. Allow awareness to evolve and mature.
4. Acknowledge the wonder of your mind as a friend.

Embark on this four-step practice of PRAA; it bears fruit. Become dedicated to developing a precious friendship with your mind. Let it evolve by taking one step at a time from wherever you are now. This action will naturally propel you farther and prepare you for future moments.

Awareness fosters more awareness. Over time, you will notice that as you become familiar with the four steps of PRAA, moving back to being friends with your mind will become natural to you. From time to time, you'll find your mind enjoying happiness. Allow yourself to bask in its delight. No need to figure out from where it came or what it means; merely enjoy.

Now, more able to befriend your mind, you are well-equipped to take the next step. In the following chapter, you will gain many healthy methods for transforming stressful situations and calming your mind. Engaging any of the methods will help disabling thoughts fade out of sight.

MAGNIFICENT MIND

Imagine your magnificent mind brimming with untapped wonder,
vast wealth
springing from supreme peace, boundless love
witness of all unfolding
silently observing with gentle, expansive awareness.

Like a slim glimmer of sunset mirrored on the ocean's face,
let all thoughts dissolve,
lessening into blips of inconsequence—
your golden mind
still, steadfast, translucent, your cherished friend.

CHAPTER 9
Effective Responses When Feeling Stressed

When our mind swirls in a whirlwind, and we feel stressed, there is no need to blame ourselves or anyone else; judgment doesn't help. Be kind.

Emotions are integral to us as humans. They are energy, a natural touchstone that helps us notice what is transpiring in our mind. Being aware of our emotional state is greatly significant. It is a decisive juncture, a turning point where making a shift is possible. This shift opens new neural pathways, full of vitality and positivity.

Once we notice fear, stress, or judgment step in, we can allow a more wholehearted perspective to surface. We can enhance the friendship with our mind by embracing our power to choose. Every time we take the option of noticing troubling thoughts or feelings and make another choice, we step closer to happiness. And every time we heal the thoughts and energy that deplete us, we step closer to happiness.

Experiment with the following methods. Practice each one. Choose the method or methods that work best for you.

EFFECTIVE RESPONSES AND METHODS

- A powerful stance to take is this: Let the notion occur that we "might" be wrong about the way we are seeing and thinking.

Pausing to consider our position fosters humility and creates spaciousness within us for a new possibility to dawn.

○ Or try this: Allow the disabling thought to glide away and dissolve as easily as releasing our next exhalation. It is as natural as unclenching a fist. When we let go, we return to being in the present, free and unfettered. Things that can hold us back at this moment are self-righteousness and the cozy security of the angst feeling. The only comfort we find in either of these options is their familiarity. Neither of them offers us joy.

○ Another powerful way to still disturbing thoughts is to bring our attention to our breath. The breath forms a bridge between the mind and body. When we breathe consciously into our heart, the mind relinquishes its possession. Become aware; allow each inhalation and exhalation to be relaxed, deepened, and slow.

○ Whether the intrusion is a thought or an uncomfortable emotion, adopting long, easeful breaths guides the mind to tranquility. We return to the present, feeling the air on our skin, the clothes on our back, and even noticing details in our physical environment. We become centered—inwardly open, with our mind and body connected, revitalized.

○ Another breath-practice that calms the mind is to breathe in for a count of five and release fully to a count of ten. Relax; do not strain. At first, a long exhalation might seem difficult. Over time and with ease, let the exhalations lengthen, making them longer than the in-breaths, until a count of ten is natural.

○ Listen to the sound the breath makes as it ebbs and flows. Our breath is the most faithful of mantras. Fastening our awareness to its unhurried rhythm, we connect once again in our heart. Then a feeling of quiet stillness emerges.

○ It is also possible to respond to a pain-filled thought as we would to a friend who has said something outrageous. We would make light of their error, knowing their true spirit. We need to do the same thing for our mind, who is also our friend and needs our friendship in a painful moment like this.

○ When having distrustful thoughts about another person, it is best to remember how we have no grasp or understanding about what they hold most dear in their heart. We do not know the struggles they may be facing. Having regard for their humanity wakes us from a harmful daze and softens our perspective.

○ Another approach would be to redirect our focus elsewhere, to thoughts that uplift our spirit. We have a full quiver of beautiful moments that soothe our soul and calm the mind. Magic happens when we recall one memory that we treasure and let its experience fill our entire being with delight. This response is as refreshing and energizing as a dip in the ocean.

Choosing any one of these methods, or a combination of them, allows disruptive thoughts to fade out of sight. They dissolve back into stillness. It allows our emotions to become balanced and more tranquil, released from being bound up in a hypnotic or adverse state.

Each time we consciously respond with positivity, we free our mind. Our power to choose expands. We build a new habit. We create space between thoughts—golden, calm spaciousness.

We shift from thinking, to a sense of self, to awareness. We discover that we have thoughts rather than believing we are the thoughts. Our mind returns to its pure state.

As we practice, our mindfulness grows; we establish a stable friendship with our mind. Our practice offers invaluable rewards and supports us during more intense times.

Our continual care and attention support the mind's capacity to become tranquil and clear, a creative, magnetic current of life. The mind responds with equipoise and functions well on our behalf. We make clear-minded decisions. Incredible abilities mature. Relationships improve. We live with more flexibility and can express a more significant percentage of the mind's great attributes. And as the mind returns to its essential nature, love, peace, and joy are waiting for us. This inner state is worth all the effort we have put forth to get here.

Our mind's genius grows ever-more-significantly potent, creating a world in which beauty, love, and harmony hold up the sky.

REFINED MIND

Imagine your refined mind awakening you from slumber,
still as a calm lake,
producing worlds of optimal choice,
realms beyond imagination.

Comprehend your immeasurable power,
free to choose your outlook, interpretations, responses.

Like the certainty of day following night,
cherish fearlessness, patient confidence,
inhaling *yes*, exhaling *thank you*.
Yes and *thank you* echoing in your rib cage again and again—

Quiet, delicate cadence
immersing you in a deep pool of tranquility.

CHAPTER 10
Sounds Flood Our Senses

We can get easily distracted, our attention captivated by media competing for our attention like blaring loudspeakers, teeming everyday activity, and internal noises that flood our mind. Continual input obscures the senses as sounds swarm with whirlwind force. And yet, inside, there is a steady, soundless space. To sit inside that soundless space and experience stillness is a balm to the ears, the mind, and our whole being.

Grandfather Twilight lives among the trees. When day is done, he closes his book, combs his beard, and puts on his jacket.

Next, he opens a wooden chest that is filled with an endless strand of pearls. He lifts the strand, takes one pearl from it, and closes the chest again.

Then, holding the pearl in his hand, Grandfather Twilight goes for a walk.

The pearl grows larger with every step. Leaves begin to whisper—little birds hush.

Gently, he gives the pearl to the silence above the sea.

Then Grandfather Twilight goes home again. He gets ready for bed. And he goes to sleep.

from *Grandfather Twilight*

Reading this story reminds me of bedtime stories with my children—our time together quieted my mind and heart from a busy day. Without stillness in our day, we would be so overwhelmed that disease could result—our nervous system frays, and the body can lose its ability to fight off sickness. Knowing how vital our well-being is, let's take time to honor the gift of listening, to hear sounds that can uplift us and improve our life.

We can't stop sounds. As we move through the world, we don't get to pick what goes through our senses. A car screeches; we hear it. We get to choose where our awareness goes and how we respond. Since we don't want to inhibit our hearing ability, we need to teach ourselves to attend to what is uplifting—what supports our well-being. We need to make choices.

Wikipedia states that many health problems are due to regular exposure to consistent, elevated sound levels. "Noise from traffic is considered by the World Health Organization to be one of the worst environmental stressors for humans. It is second only to air pollution. Elevated noise can cause hearing impairment, tinnitus, heart disease, sleep disturbance, and changes in the immune system."

What goes through our ears affects our mind, our heart, and our health. Therefore, being conscious of what we hear is essential to a healthy life. Just as the body needs rest, so, too, does the mind. We fulfill that need with deep sleep. And during the day, our ears and mind need to have relaxing moments as well.

We could consider being selective about the sounds we take in. Not all the sounds that people and the world make are for us to absorb or respond to—listening to negativity, demeaning words, or harsh tones affects our state. Those sounds can be external to us from the media or our circle of family, coworkers, and friends. Or they can be internal, adverse repetitions resounding inside due to our way of thinking.

Since sounds have a profound effect on our mind, to enhance the mind's health, we can become more aware and then consciously choose where we put our attention.

Think about this: If you had the very best measurement tools to determine the health of your mind, what would be your mind's health care report?

1. What kind of care is needed?
2. Does it need routine, urgent, or emergency care?
3. How might resting the mind be beneficial?

We can protect and maintain our mind's and body's strength by listening to inspiring sounds. We owe it to ourselves, our family, our coworkers, and our pets to pause in our day and allow our mind to be in a good state by rejuvenating it with soothing sounds. Uplifting music, bird songs, children laughing, and the natural world's many beautiful sounds restore and calm. As we slow down and listen with quiet awareness, we might even notice a slight breeze murmuring through the trees, whispering our name. All those pure sounds return us to our heart, nurture our senses, and help us get through difficult times. The mind and body increase in vitality.

Imagine Divine Sound spawning multitudes of variations—
unmistakable as a thunderstorm blasting across the sky,
the ocean crashing against the shore,
raindrops dancing on the roof,
jackhammers cracking rock, the roar of traffic,

church bells chiming,
children playing in the schoolyard, bees humming their tunes,
muted footsteps of an ant carrying dinner back to her colony.

Kabir sings: "The Lord can hear the anklets that ring on the delicate feet of an ant as it walks." Can you imagine how the Lord must love to listen with rapt attention to Kabir's poetry?

Symphonies flood your mind—
to-do lists, meaningless chatter,
replays of the latest movie hits,
unsettled squabbles,
thoughts of failure or self-importance,

the mantra your breath repeats as it gently flows in and out,
enchanting words your heart longs to speak—
most profound of all, silence.

What you long to hear is beyond the senses. Whenever it is possible, day in and day out, make time for spacious stillness. Allow your mind to rest in its true nature. Gently turn your focus within, listen to the restful sound of silence—imagine you and your mind lounging in a hammock free from thoughts, doing nothing. Taste the sweetness of quiet within; experience peacefulness.

How enchanting it is to visit the tranquility of the luminous space within, where you can almost hear the pulsing in your own heart whispering, *OM*.

CHAPTER 11

Exquisite Symphony

Information passes between people in many ways. We can see it written or expressed in gestures. There is communication that involves dialogue. And communication is best when it involves more than just our physical senses.

As we keep good company and let our whole being become absorbed in sweet sounds, nourishing sounds, we will fill with unfathomable love, peace, and joy. We will be more attuned to others—present and able to hear what others would like us to hear. Listening creates connection. As the mind quiets, we will be able to listen to the messages people's hearts are giving, perhaps even the intent and sentiments below and between the spoken words.

Our ears will easily wrap around listening in ways similar to how forest life interacts, raindrops transmit cloud-speak, and animals relate. If you have a pet, you experience that ability to hear your pet communicating. Parents' hearing is acute, involving more than the ears. They sense their infant's needs—a mother's milk comes even before the child cries.

When communicating consciously, the listener and speaker are in a mutual dance exchanging fluent, graceful words, phrases, feelings, meaning. It becomes a sacred exchange of heart energy. Our listening receptors invite the speaker to go on, move deeper, tell more. Each person is leaning in to offer and receive from each other, ready to be refashioned by what transpires.

In Maria Popova's *Brain Pickings* article about Ursula Le Guin, she explores with Ursula what it means to hear another person. They focused on a marvelous essay called "Telling Is Listening."

Le Guin notes, "The magic of human communication is that something other than mere information is being transmitted—something more intangible yet more real."

People and speech vibrate, pulsate. While a person is speaking and we listen with our whole being, we can hear the sound vibration of love enveloping their words.

When their words pass through our ears and enter our heart, we can delight in and enjoy the person. Together, our minds and hearts pulsate, communicating volumes more than mere information. As listeners and speakers, we become entrained. States, energy, and feelings interchange. And when done with awareness, communication can reshape our way of seeing, thinking, being.

There is a story about listening with our whole being that I love—it is still implanted in my heart, even though I read it forty years ago. It is a story of a doctor with his patient. They spoke no words, and yet the most profound communication happened.

In the book *How Can I Help*, Paul Gorman relates this story of the Dalai Lama's physician:

At precisely 6 o'clock Yeshi Dhonden materializes. A short, golden, barrelly man dressed in a sleeveless robe of saffron and maroon, his scalp is shaven, and the only visible hair is a scanty black line above each hooded eye.

Yeshi Dhonden, we are told, will examine a patient. He steps to the bedside. For a long time, he gazes at the patient, favoring no part of the body with his eyes, but seeming to fix his glance above the supine form. At last, he takes the patient's hand, raising it in both of his own.

Now he bends over the bed, in a kind of crouching stance, his head drawn down into the collar of his robe. His eyes are closed as he feels for her pulse. In a moment he has found the spot. And for the next half hour, he remains thus, suspended above the patient, like some exotic golden bird with folded wings, holding the pulse of the woman beneath his fingers, cradling her hand in his.

Their hands are joined in a correspondence that is exclusive, intimate, his fingertips receiving the voice of her sick body.

All at once, I am envious. Not of him. Not of Yeshi Dhonden for his gift of beauty and holiness, but of her. I want to be held like that. Touched so. Received.

As the doctor goes to leave the room, the patient touches her wrist, offering silent thanks.

To be received with this much patience, kindness, care, and respect, to receive another with this much patience, kindness, care, and respect is sacred.

Receptivity and presence create healthy communication, healthy relationships, beauty.

"This event of speech," Le Guin argues, "is the most potent form of entrainment we humans have—and the intimate tango of speaking and listening is the stuff of great power and great magic."

Each time we offer our respect, we cause waves of love to flow into the world.

May we always speak gracious words and hear glorious sounds.

A MYSTERY

Imagine affable acceptance—shoulders relaxed,
walking side by side, connected, interested—
spacious breadth for another to ponder, to speak.

Just as moonlight bathes weary souls,
your presence soothes hearts,
communicating caring,
deep respect, shelter, trust.

Sympathetic rhythm ushers you
ever so gently into communion, rapport
hearts, minds, souls harmonized, unified—attuned.

CHAPTER 12

Magic

There are many different paths for investigating truth: metaphorical, philosophical, scientific, spiritual, and from a global humanitarian perspective, to mention a few.

In the book (and movie) *Tuesdays with Morrie*, we meet Morrie, a thoughtful man nearing the end of his life. He shares his understanding of the essential things of life through stories and metaphors with a philosophical bent.

"I heard a nice little story the other day," Morrie says. He closes his eyes for a moment, and I wait.

"Okay. The story is about a little wave, bobbing along in the ocean, having a grand old time. He's enjoying the wind and the fresh air—until he notices the other waves in front of him, crashing against the shore."

"My God, this is terrible," the wave says. "Look what's going to happen to me!"

Then along comes another wave. It sees the first wave, looking grim, and it says to him, "Why do you look so sad?"

The first wave says, "You don't understand! We're all going to crash! All of us waves are going to be nothing! Isn't it terrible?"

The second wave says, "No, you don't understand. You're not a wave; you're part of the ocean."

I smile.

Morrie closes his eyes again. "Part of the ocean," he says, "part of the ocean."

What if Morrie's inner experience of becoming part of the ocean is magic?

Discovering the meaning of things is the pursuit and discipline of philosophy. It is a love of wisdom. It questions beliefs and thoughts to solve questions and problems relevant in our lives. Who am I? Why am I here? Philosophy helps us think about the interrelationship of things in ways we may not previously have considered.

Dr. C. Terry Warner is a contemporary philosopher whose knowledge has had a significant impact on thinking. In his book *Bonds That Make Us Free*, he writes, "To the degree that we become receptive and responsive to the truth, life will keep instructing us. It will teach us all sorts of fresh things about matters we thought we already understood."

There seems to be a recurrent theme in life that points us toward being receptive to the "fresh things" that Dr. Warner mentions. We see this in the field of science, as well. Scientists update understanding by exploring, studying, and discovering more and more about the interplay of the forces of the universe. Science has evidence that surprises.

A world leader in physics, Nassim Haramein has found that we need new mathematical models to solve what can be observed but not understood. His research and discoveries have produced the unified field theory to reconcile some of the most significant discrepancies in current scientific understanding. His point of view bridges ancient spirituality with cutting-edge physics.

HOW VARIOUS PERSPECTIVES SHED LIGHT ON MAGIC

When any of us experiences a moment that seems like magic, it often feels both familiar and foreign. It surprises us. We've been here before but can't remember how we got here. There is a comforting homecoming quality to it—usually wondrous and freeing. How did we stray from this place? How could we have been so close and yet missed it? Perhaps we missed it because this not-easily-described element cannot be seen or held in our hand; it is a felt sense. And even though it has this subtlety, it is as real as the nose on our face.

The magic arises from a place beyond our mind and is recognized when we are in tune with it, hidden when we are not present to it. Another name for this magic could be the "oneness" that we all are: some deep-rooted experience of being one soul, one heart, one rhythm pulsing in everything.

It is sometimes puzzling to hold two realities; we know that we are us, separate and uniquely individual, while also having experiences of oneness with others. A classic example of this is meeting someone for the first time but immediately feeling one with them; we know them. Or another example: while thinking about a person we haven't seen or heard from for years, they call. In these examples, we feel connected in surprising ways.

How does that happen? In those moments, there is something more that enters our field of possibility. Dr. Warner reminds us that life "will teach us all sorts of fresh things about matters we thought we already understood."

What feels normal or usual to us seems to slip away, making room for the unexpected. That is why we refer to it as magic. It has a quality a little like humor. It catches us off guard or outside of what we anticipate. At those moments, our heart's energy is more prominent than the facts stored in our mind. The clear distinctions with which we have defined the world shift. There isn't the usual delineation of where we end and another begins. In those moments, we are more than the person we have defined ourselves to be.

Over 30 years ago, a friend and I discussed a shared desire to engage in a ritual of forgiveness to wash away years of regret. Soon after expressing that wish, we both happened to be in Arizona at the same time.

Before meeting at the Grand Canyon, we each had time to gather thoughts and precious items for our experience. When we met together at the rim, awed by its vast depth, we knew it could hold all we were ready to release and consign to it. We meditated, wept for the hurts we had done to others, let go of the pain we held tightly to and blamed others for, and cleared away many of life's unfinished transactions—those that had previously weighed us down.

Now, with our hearts much lighter, we gave gifts to the canyon. Along with tears, we offered sage, cornmeal, and flower petals carried by the wind. Our hearts overflowed with peace, contentment, jubilation. Feeling absolved, we stretched our arms wide, hands opened to the sky in thanksgiving. To our surprise, birds came and sat on our hands. It seemed as if nature itself was participating in our simple ritual performed at its rim. How harmonious the world felt, one harmonic symphony, one consciousness.

My friend and I experienced an unusual and memorable occasion. Native American people guide their lives with this deep understanding and respect—oneness with the sun, the moon, the earth, and all its creatures. Nature surrounds them as living, beautiful, vital companions. They listen to what the natural world speaks and give thanks for all that is offered. They might describe their connectedness this way: the circle of creation is one continuous relationship, with all my relations sharing the same breath, the same heartbeat.

IT IS LOVE

The experience of oneness is a taste of what feels most real to us. It is love. The love we are discussing is not feelings, infatuation, or romantic love. Instead, it is a mysterious unbridled state that is not only alive in us but resounds in every particle of the universe. It is a pure and infinitely expansive state.

Love is our essential nature. Its memory is always echoing inside us. It creates a longing to be noticed and to experience itself. Like a sound pulse that dolphins send out and receive in the water, we feel or hear love's resonance within us and long to be absorbed in it.

I appreciate and look forward to receiving the Make-A-Wish bulletin. It contains stories of wishes granted to children with life-threatening conditions. Here are three accounts I have read of young boys making and receiving wishes.

J'Len, four years old, wants to be a policeman, like his dad. He is in full uniform, including the badge. He stands tall and proud. He is being sworn in as a police officer. "I promise to always do what is right, help others when I can, and obey my parents." J'Len proudly receives an award for bravery.

Nine-year-old Aidan said, "I wish to be a penguin keeper, because I was born loving penguins." In the middle of his wish coming true, Aidan turns to his mom and says, "Mom, I can't stop smiling. My face is starting to hurt."

Liam, age ten, spends most of his time in bed. He wants to meet the "real guys" behind his favorite video game, Call of Duty. He got to sit in a Blackhawk helicopter and learn skills in the simulators. At a ceremony, he receives a standing ovation, with sixty Army members saluting him. They give him badges right off their uniforms, which sticks in his memory long after the event. The "real guys" made him one of them.

The boys' fulfilled wishes were more than any of them could have imagined. They were thrilled. It was also over-the-top amazing for all the people involved in granting the wishes. Each one of their hearts was blown open with love and gratitude for these boys and their courage. The wish-granters received a taste of the magic of oneness.

Perhaps our stories of feeling one with another person are not that dramatic, but we have them. They are stored inside. Look now at one of yours:

- Think back to when your heart opened wide to someone. You might know them, or not. (Perhaps they are a friend's relative or their story was in the news.)
- Revisit your heart-opening experience now. Where were you? What were the circumstances?
- Recall it; more than just thinking about it, let yourself recapture the experience in your heart. What are you feeling now? . . . In your heart? . . . In your body?
- Can you allow yourself to relax even more into the feelings? . . . Immerse yourself.

Even though this event happened in the past, it is present inside your heart at this moment. Is this magic? Is what we hold so dear to us embedded deeply within our heart, waiting for us to embrace it again?

OPENING OUR HEART TO LOVE LETS IN ONENESS

Humans have basic needs—love, acceptance, belonging—oneness. Our hearts urge us to fulfill our longing. We search for it unceasingly. Our minds keep busy, looking outside, everywhere, for satisfaction.

It is why we are so happy and deeply content when we experience resonance with a piece of music, a profound moment in nature, a healed relationship, or a spiritual encounter. Our whole being relaxes; our heart exclaims "yes," affirming how everything feels right, even perfect. We have recognized that the glorious experiences we desire exist inside. Once more, internal, energetic connections are reestablished and strengthened. These moments give us the experience of arriving back home, inside our heart, to what we know and trust as most real.

Imagine the All-Embracing One
wrapping a bear hug around humankind,
smiling from ear to ear with complete acceptance,
offering new vision to see what has been invisible.

Like a child bursting with joyful expectation,
be unafraid, full of wonder and daring,
magically transported to a land where lone hearts dissolve
into a glorious, gorgeous, shimmering light.

Eyes and heart dazzled by the brilliance,
you breathlessly,
eagerly enter paradise to roam the blissful realm of oneness.

This most subtle and continuous pulse of love awakens and manifests every moment new and fresh. It beats in our heart, pulses through our veins, blinks our eyes, sings through the wind, throbs beneath the earth, roars on the ocean floor, and becomes myriad things and experiences, including the kindness of the people in our lives. The more we embrace these magical happenings and respond with wonder, the more we will come to know oneness and experience "one" heart.

CHAPTER 13
Love Turns the Key

Each breath is a new beginning, a fresh start, a moment when creation is alive and clarity is possible. Breath and love transport us magically to freedom. So powerful and potent, love can shake loose habits and tendencies that have bound us. This innate love we all experience delivers us to an expanded state of possibilities. In this state, we may even behave in unlikely ways, ways that surprise us and others.

Many have heard the story circulated on the internet about one race years ago at a Special Olympics event.

As the children were running, one child tripped and fell. All the other children racing ahead heard whimpering. They stopped their forward course and went back. They picked up the fallen child. Then they took each other's hands and ran together toward the finish line.

Children's hearts are spontaneous. They can express their love with so much enthusiasm. They do not play by rules or second-guess their hearts.

In the story, the children innocently and quickly saw with their hearts what to do: help the fallen child. Without hesitation, these runners' hearts responded to something much grander than a medal for being first. No one lost; the whole group won and felt overjoyed from listening and responding to their hearts.

In daily life, love's magnetic attraction leads us to discover friends and fall in love. We recognize love's whisper. We enter relationships, even become committed, because we are deeply aligned, matched like a puzzle piece to another person, and we believe, "That's it, that's what I have been looking for; I have found it."

And then when our chosen person doesn't respond the way we want, perhaps doesn't understand us or points out our imperfections, we push them away, saying, "You are wrong. You don't know me. You don't love me." We turn away from the magic. We become numb to the oneness of love pulsing inside us, between us. We begin another quest to search for the magic that is already standing next to us. How silly we are.

My friend and business partner, Sharon, shares this story:

When I have pulled away from others, I am so self-focused that I literally cannot see anything but myself. I have no ears, no flexibility, no heart, no grace. I was having a conversation with my friend Amy about something in the news. She was in-sensitive. I felt that she was missing the big picture. The voice in my head said, "I can't believe she is so blind. She's not as smart or aware as I had thought. I don't want to spend much time with her." Focused on my superiority, I stopped seeing or even being with Amy. Now, who was insensitive?

There are many other ways we implant wedges of varying sizes between us and the people in our lives. See if you can name a few. They might look small, like an annoyance or displeasure. They might be more active, like bargaining, keeping score, withholding, or being a martyr. They are recognizable because we would be embarrassed to admit them in public.

All these ways of feeling separate from others are self-absorbed and a long way from oneness. They do not help us resolve the issue, feel closer, or move on. They generate only negative energy. These ways of feeling separate are very human. We all do them.

Love flows from a limitless wellspring. It has more stability than the habits and fortresses of separation built up over generations of humanity.

ELIMINATE UNHELPFUL WAYS OF RELATING

We must stop being careless or permissive with ourselves, letting ourselves off the hook. Destructive patterns indeed inhibit sharing the love in our heart.

A client who is a former heart surgeon told me about constrictive pericarditis, a term which means there is scar tissue around the heart—like clamps that constrict it. Inflammation causes the heart's covering to become thick and rigid, making it hard for the heart to stretch correctly when it beats. As a result, the heart chambers do not fill up with enough blood. This condition prevents the heart muscle from expanding and instead tightens the muscle. A heart surgeon does surgery to dissect away the scar tissue that is squeezing the heart.

Let's think about this heart condition as a metaphor for our resistance to or defensiveness with others. Our dislike of someone or judgment of their behavior tightens up our thoughts and feelings toward them. We are mentally, emotionally squeezing our heart and not allowing it to expand. It is very much like saying, "I don't want to make room for you." We become rigid and inflexible. We tell any story we can to keep this tragic tale alive. We excuse and justify our behavior, often blaming the other person for causing the pain and heartache we feel.

UNCONSCIOUS

Our wrong thinking sedates us, and we do not even know it. It is as if we are in a daze, systematically putting clamps in place one by one, sometimes unconsciously—however, every clamp limits love, joy, and spontaneity. We steadily squeeze the life out of our heart and out of relationships.

When we haven't made space in ourselves to receive a person, we step away from them in our heart. We think if we disconnect and dismiss them, we will be safe. Instead, our decision limits us. Whether it is with coworkers, friends, family, or neighbors, our thoughts, actions, and attitudes judge rather than understand and embrace. We remain a wave, afraid to merge with the ocean.

I was already seated at an event as attendees were entering. I was people-watching and somehow noticed that my watching wasn't harmless. All around the edges were my thoughts, opinions, comparisons, judgments, and separateness.

Then, in an instant, catching myself, I woke up. This new thought appeared—this time as a whisper from my heart: You have no idea what is in the heart of each person. Teary-eyed, I allowed my heart to soften.

Given fresh vision, I began to see tender hearts entering the room, and I experienced "all my relations," as the Native Americans say. That experience felt sacred.

"Oneness" is an incredible stance to adopt. Oneness and love matter and are the keys to transforming relationships. In relating to others, we have all had moments of knowing this powerfully connected feeling, this oneness. Perhaps it was at the birth of a child, in celebrating a dear friend's long-awaited success, or in an everyday experience, such as being deeply touched by a person's unexpected kindness.

I was living across the globe from home, family, and friends. I had a powerful dream. And the next time I called the States to speak with a friend, I found they had had the identical dream.

We felt "one" not only in the moment during that realization but also connected through time and space.

ONENESS, MAGIC, LOVE BECOME INDISTINGUISHABLE

Moments of love sometimes arise from shared values, passions, or sacred experiences, sometimes in response to external situations, like sitting shiva with a dear friend. When we nurture our internal expansion of oneness, love springs naturally and unsolicited from deep within our heart. We can become so fluent that love is our automatic response to others. No matter what another person's state may be, our rootedness in being "one" heart with them will outweigh any resistance in us.

The true definition of vulnerability with another person is a state of fearlessness, a powerful perspective that causes us to trust in ourselves and others. No longer do we need to shield our heart to protect ourselves. As our natural state of love becomes more constant, shifting our heart in difficult moments becomes easier. A Native American chant can escort us to this space now.

Relax into your breath, inhaling softly and exhaling slowly, with ease. When you are ready, gently bring your awareness to your heart. You might like to place your hand or hands lightly over your physical heart to increase awareness. You may even notice or hear the heart's cadence. Take your time.

Now, allow your heart to fill with the radiant light of this Navajo chant:

This that is beautiful, it shows my way.
This that is beautiful, it shows my way.
Before me is beautiful, it shows my way.
Behind me is beautiful, it shows my way.

This that is beautiful, it shows my way.
Above me is beautiful, it shows my way.
Below me is beautiful, it shows my way.
This that is beautiful, it shows my way.
This that is beautiful, it shows my way.

Deep inside your heart reside boundless love, splendid power, and vast wisdom. Immerse yourself. Beauty surrounds you and enfolds you in an ocean of spacious serenity. Let all your thoughts dissolve into expansive and luminous stillness, and enter oneness. Dwell here for a few moments.

Absorbed in this place of wonder, notice your experience.

We are on life's journey to uncover all we have not seen; in the same way, philosophy expands our thinking, and the sciences keep discovering more about the universe. As we peel back layers of assumptions and division, we will experience the love that has been there all along. It will become apparent how being deaf to our heart's whispers impacts our relationships. When we look in the right way, we will find the answers.

Here is a tale from a compilation of humorous oral stories handed down about Mullah Nasrudin. The title *mullah* (or *mulla*) is used as a term of respect for a man thought to be very wise. However, this beloved character is known throughout the Middle East and Central Asia, by children and adults alike, for his antics. Much of the time, he is the fool making us laugh at his lack of common sense or outrageousness.
Sometimes he reveals a deeper truth about our lives.

Someone saw Nasrudin searching for something on the ground.

"What have you lost, Mulla?" he asked.

"My key," said the Mulla. So, they both went down on their knees looking for it.

After a time, the other man asked, "Where exactly did you drop it?"

"In my own house."

"Then why are you looking here?"

"There is more light here than inside my own house."

from *The Exploits of the Incomparable Mulla Nasrudin*

Isn't it great that over and over in our daily lives, even when we have lost the key, something as profound as the magic of love's oneness knocks again at our awareness? A coworker stops to chat; our child wants us to play; the weather outside is glorious; we receive three happy texts from the same person; all are bidding us to look in the right place, to return to our heart.

Let's turn our attention to someone that might be knocking for entrance to our heart. Please recall a person whom you might be overlooking, a person who longs for you to appreciate them.

- o Do you feel their hunger? Is it something they say? How is their behavior begging for your attention?
- o Could it be a whisper you hear in your heart?
- o Can you recognize the longing in their heart?
- o What are their great qualities? How have you seen love shine through them?
- o In what ways are they more like you than different?
- o How can you let them know they are worthy of your love?

At this moment, put aside all the questions and answers. Reverently hold this thought. Know that the same love that exists in your heart exists in their heart as well.

Now you are ready to share with them whatever is in your heart: possibly a story or an exchange that has touched you.

What if each of us could become aware of our own and other people's innate beauty and goodness? What if we could see the similarities in all people, even those who live far away or live by different values and beliefs? What if we got good at seeing past our differences to our shared humanity? How might our lives and the whole world change?

We built a robust infrastructure. We honed our awareness and became friends with our breath and our mind. With deep appreciation for our generous heart, love, and oneness, we are ready to delve into the compelling topic of relationships.

The Zen Buddhist monk Thich Nhat Hanh explains, "We are here to awaken from the illusion of our separateness."

MYSTICAL MAGIC

Better than pulling a nose-twitching rabbit
out of a magician's hat,
your ability to create awe far exceeds trickery
and doesn't need a hat.
Your secret magic: potent
yet imperceptible melts fear, worry, sorrow—

Breath sweeping through you
kindles effervescent sparks,
bestows spaciousness, connection,
rousing edge-of-seat anticipation.

Extraordinary openheartedness seeps
through cracks in perceptions,
between words, thoughts, feelings—
prunes withered beliefs and patterns of behaviors.

Your gentle regard envelops
another's joy, pain, dreams, beauty.
Consenting to free fall together,
hearts meld, hastening sweet oneness.

Vulnerability of this highest order
transforms ordinary into mystical magic—
unexpected amazement,
two hearts,
one splendid brilliance.

CHAPTER 14
Relationships Matter

Whether speaking with a parent or spouse, with leaders or teams in an organization, I find that when those I am speaking with are in a healthy relationship with the people involved, the solutions they are searching for happen quickly, naturally. Relationships matter to every one of us. Some of our relationships are strong as steel; others might be fragile.

> In 1975 Muhammad Ali was invited to talk to a group of Harvard students. Someone in the crowd shouted, "Give us a poem, Muhammad." He paused for a moment, looked up, and said: "Me. We."
>
> from *Jim Carroll's Blog*

I love the simplicity and the profundity of Ali's poem. Once we know, love, and are kind to ourselves, we start to experience that there is no "other"; all of us are connected, experiencing one precious breath.

Our relationships form our lives' context, weaving together the tapestry of our experiences. We gravitate toward people we love and care about, people who add joy and laughter to our lives. Relationships that provide safety and trust buoy us up. We want that; we long for great connections.

Then there are people that we desperately want to respect us, people that make us bite our lips or feel huge knots in our bellies, and perhaps people we won't let near us. Whether we see people as a pain in our side or a splendid gift in our lives, they matter. However, we can operate in a mindless state or delude ourselves regarding how we are in relationship with others.

When we are not in sync with our heart's endearing qualities and/or we are not happily linked to the people in our lives, our world does not feel right. When our mind is in charge, genuine connection isn't possible; we are heart-poor, and we establish little mutuality. So it isn't only that we need people in our life; it is essential that we are in healthy relationships with them. When we care for people, our connections become strong. Having healthy relationships makes all the difference in the quality of our life.

WHICH RELATIONSHIPS MATTER?

In researching this topic, most websites focused on relationships are speaking about intimate relationships. That is assuredly a high priority for most people, a most significant category of relationship. Bonds of trust and affection produce an entire range of emotions and satisfaction.

Dr. Vivek Murthy, the former surgeon general of the United States, adds two more categories of connection that are fundamental. He states that relationships (1) of quality friendships and companionships and (2) where we feel part of a community with others are crucial. In a community, we have similar convictions, purpose, and principles. When we are rich in all three of these categories (intimate, friendship, like-minded community relationships), we experience wholeness, a sense of belonging, feeling accepted and valued for who we are.

Sometimes we relate better with people in one category than another due to our history, disposition, and sense of self. However, it is desirable to create a relationship-rich life. When we are relationship-poor, loneliness becomes a significant danger to health. As a matter of fact, Dr. Murthy's research established that loneliness is the most prevalent disease in America. In his book *Together*, he reveals how authentic human connection is essential for physical, mental, and emotional health.

Loneliness is so difficult to fathom in the twenty-first century, yet it is more common than smoking and far more harmful as a health hazard.

WHAT IS ESSENTIAL FOR HEALTHY RELATIONSHIPS?

To connect with others, we need to have a quality relationship with ourselves, truly value ourselves, and know we are worthy of love and respect. In an interview, Dr. Murthy expressed how true belonging can't happen unless we belong to ourselves. His statement confirms my belief about the importance of feeling kindly toward ourselves.

Our heart needs to be accessible to us. We must become experienced at catching our thoughts, seeing how we view ourselves. When we respect and love ourselves, we can honestly meet another person, be with them, and hear them. Our heart is ready to engage with them. Otherwise, disconnection happens, particularly when feelings of "less than," shame, or degrees of deficiency exist. While finding fault with ourselves, we also unconsciously begin fault-finding in others, often adding judgment or blame.

A dear friend of mine reminded me of a beautiful Japanese art form that came about to reinforce and beautify imperfect or broken ceramic. This gold-mending process, called *Kintsugi*, visually transforms defects and imperfections into art while creating a unique, more robust piece. The gold lines become part of the history of the piece.

Kintsugi can be a metaphor for our life. It is easy to be self-critical and dwell on what isn't perfect—what we don't like about ourselves. Disapproval can be a slippery slope. Instead, we can take steps to love what we consider our brokenness. We can say no, not true, and take hold of the certainty of our worth, our goodness. We can appreciate what is good and powerful about us through gold-mending our flaws and pain. This decision helps us be authentic, even more beautiful, and resilient.

SELF-LOVE

Like daylight swallows darkness,
consciously stroll past loneliness and self-doubt,
release hurtful opinions, judgments, and feeling snail-small.

Embrace truth—
Your heart is the purest, robust spirit.
Prepare to look with fresh eyes—banishing limiting stories, shame.

Ease your mind,
enter a field of resilient possibilities—a new narrative.
Celebrate the exquisite marvel—

YOU
shimmering light, gods' and goddesses' stunning design,
goodness, blessedness.

Welcome home!
Spin, frolic, sing among honey-scented blossoms
alive to your precious self.

CHAPTER 15

Swimming in a River of Relationships

In the past, Simone, a client of mine, found herself frustrated and perturbed by people expecting her to drop what she was doing and help them. Step by step through coaching, Simone journeyed to more loving moments and found how tender life is when her heart opens to others.

> I've been practicing seeing and caring more for the people around me. Last week I went to Trader Joe's with my children. I needed to buy olive oil.
>
> An old man, who was almost invisible, was standing by the olive oil shelf. Standing close to him, I heard him say something. Instead of saying in my mind, What's this guy doing? I can't be bothered; I'm busy, I said, "What did you say?"
>
> He said ever so slightly, "I am having a stroke; I cannot move; call 911."
>
> My heart swells at this opportunity for being human.
>
> Yes, I got him help; I stood by him until someone else could help. My kids were pretty much oblivious because they were near the tasting station.

Once we belong to ourselves, we can wholeheartedly be with others. We can comfortably offer, receive, and accept love and develop trust and friendship.

We know what it is like to treasure someone dear to us; they occupy a special place in our heart. In some ways, those we embrace feel like a part of us. We share a sacred space. We consider them and what they are going through. We care, give, and receive love and kindness. We pardon their forgetfulness or discourtesy.

We also experience that seamlessness when tragedy strikes anywhere in the world. Compassion almost instantaneously engulfs our heart. We reach out.

People occupy our mind and heart, even when what we are doing or thinking feels independent of others. Our very sustenance relies on a cadre of people, sometimes even from faraway places. Yes, people are integral to the life we live from day to day. Who we are in each relationship needs our attention, a caring eye, a willingness to evolve.

When we are fully alive in our heart, we see people and open to them. We sense their humanity and have impressions and feelings about how to be with them and respond.

How we engage in relationships provides a snapshot of how we connect with ourselves.

ARE WE AWARE?

Our intuition might say not to interfere by giving our opinion. Do we remain silent? Do we respect and trust the person or group's integrity to figure out their situation? Or do we disregard our sense and offer advice, not even aware of veiled thoughts or judgments that we might have? Perhaps we think it would be easier or faster to tell them. Or we may have an underlying need to position ourselves as the one who has the answers or can rescue them. Do we believe the people in our lives are competent? Are we aware?

When we notice someone experiencing overwhelm during our workday, we might rush to transact business rather than simply being with them for a moment. It is easy to be on autopilot, with many to-dos rumbling and billowing as they compete for our attention. Like clouds in the sky, our thoughts are in constant play. Accomplishing what is on our mind and checking off our at-hand tasks become more imperative than the person standing before us. We are insensitive and anesthetized to what is needed, even though our heart has glimpsed their stress. Are we aware?

Have you told someone you wanted to hear their story and then didn't truly listen? We already had in our mind what they were going to say, and we spaced out, occupying our mind with more interesting things. We run from being present—being open to another. After all, we already know them and their story. Are we aware?

There have been moments when we might even feel an impulse to help someone. On second thought, we hurry by as quickly as butter melts in the desert sun. It is easy for us to scurry past without getting involved. We're busy—don't have time. We give ourselves an excuse.

Honestly, we each have a deep commitment to being kind and thoughtful, and yet we can spend much time comparing, thinking in terms of differences—descriptive pairs of contrary, contrasting labels, like good or bad, right or wrong, kind or mean, rich or poor, smart or slow. Judgments bog us down, separate rather than connect us to others. They fling kindness off to the side. They stifle our heart. Are we aware?

Only the mind's trickery causes us to believe other people are our measuring rods instead of knowing that the warmth in our own heart is our best measure. The values we hold about how we truly want to live in this world will get challenged repeatedly. Can we hold firm to and live our values? How conscious are we? How aware?

Can we offer kindness wherever love is not available or missing? Or do we get obsessed with keeping score in tit-for-tat reckonings because of what someone may have said or done?

On the other hand, we can be rock-solid sure that how we envision and think about another person is valid. We might think they don't deserve our caring. We can clutch onto a feeling of rightness about who we believe they are and how they impact our lives. We bet our lives on it, and that is what causes pain and suffering. People appear to be separate from us only when we don't have access to our heart. The certainty of our conviction traps us, weakens our heart, and leaves us sad and lonely.

Moreover, when we put our complete attention on any single thought, we bind ourselves to it. It fills us up and excludes any other awareness. It becomes more robust as we feed it, and then it becomes solid, like concrete. Once that happens, it is harder to let it go; we become deaf to our heart's guidance. Are we aware?

No matter what we think about others or ourselves, it is a fleeting fancy. We know that we have both praised ourselves and cursed ourselves. In each moment, whether we think we are grand or imperfect, we compare ourselves to a norm we have constructed in our mind relative to others. Our explanation of who we are differentiates us. We believe it adds credibility to our reality. And attachment to that reality, unfortunately, obstructs awareness, genuine listening, and any possibility of appreciating the other person.

Mulling over these scenarios is a little like turning our mind inside out, seeing and hearing nuances in our thoughts and behaviors that we may have missed as we rushed from thing to thing, thought to thought, being very busy or very sure. Oh, but noticing is crucial. There is great benefit in understanding what lies beneath our thoughts.

WHO WE ARE IS WHO WE ARE WITH OTHERS

All things change when we open our heart to see and listen. Understanding ourselves offers a whole different idea of who we can become as a person and how we can contribute to our relationships. Our joy and sanity are in direct proportion to the respect we have for others. Tuning into what our heart is telling us is a noble occupation. The heart's wisdom teaches us how to be present, drop unhelpful stories, and graciously be with a person. The more we allow ourselves to see and evolve, the more content we will be.

As we approach people warmheartedly, they feel safe, and relationships grow and thrive. In the next chapters, we will explore how to invite harmony and peace, especially when relationships become complicated.

For now, remember to honor yourself, recalling unquestionable truth and nourishing the pure love and light that you are.

SURRENDER

Imagine a sublime melody of "I Am,"
bountiful as noonday light
pulsing within you,
resounding throughout creation.

Like cooling ocean waves spilling over you,
experience yourself becoming fully drenched—
succumb—give in,
receive undeniable pure infinite love.

Gently lower your eyelids, reverently listen
as your heart whispers

      I AM

           I AM

                I AM

CHAPTER 16
No Need to Struggle

We all want to get through the difficult moments we encounter with another person. We don't like it when awkwardness happens between us. How do we navigate those waters? How do we maneuver successfully through uncomfortable interactions—the smallest to the most troubling—that occur in our lives?

RESILIENCE IS ATTAINABLE, NOT ONLY A WISH

Wouldn't it be great to have our relationships filled with respect, serenity, success, and satisfaction all tied up with a bow? It is truly possible. What a gift we can give ourselves and others.

So how can we remedy situations that are challenging? Perhaps you think that I will tell you to give in, and you are afraid you'll be manipulated or abused. I will not do anything like that. No need for you to worry about giving in or being walked on. Instead, you can be with others powerfully and work together harmoniously. I assume you would want that for yourself, as I did.

Resilience is a muscle; it needs to be developed. It takes time and a concerted effort. We develop resilience by meeting each challenge with our pure heart and courage. With grace, courage, and humility, we learn more each time we put forth an effort to approach life from a heart and mind at peace. When we've worked through the challenge with grace, we witness the presence of our courage. That's how resilience is developed.

I will share with you one of my own stories that increased my heart at peace, my courage, and my resilience.

UNSUSPECTING MOMENTS BRING OPPORTUNITY

There was a team doing a project together. I was a participant in what became a painful group interaction. We all had the same goal but different ideas about how to achieve it. One person felt in charge and took over. He had a detailed plan that he wanted us to carry out precisely. He was uncompromising in his thinking and not collaborative. His self-appointed authority made me frustrated.

Burning inside, I felt myself wanting to push against him. I was no longer listening or caring. These thoughts surfaced: "Who put you in charge? I am capable. I know how to do this. Go ahead, do it yourself. You have such a 'better than' attitude."

Do similar comments ever flit through your mind? For me, they appeared with the speed of light. Although that day I did not say them, I am sure my disposition conveyed my feelings. Unfortunately, sometimes I have said hurtful words out loud, which only adds more stress.

Let's address a similar situation you may face. We will look through a lens that can be helpful. Choose one stressful circumstance, whether it is mild, like this one, or just a bit more stressful. To get the most out of the chapter, practice on a smaller irritation and then apply the learning to larger issues. I suggest that as you read, you participate with each step.

STEP ONE: CHECK YOUR MENTAL AND EMOTIONAL STATE

First and most importantly, we need to notice our mental and emotional state. Once enrolled in stinging interactions, our thoughts trigger emotions, and emotions trigger more thoughts. We might become aware of physical tightness—our stomach or jaw clenched, shoulders tightened, or tension elsewhere in our body.

When we are on automatic, not watchful, or choose to stay contracted, we lose our ability to be flexible. We shut down. We become unreliable narrators of our own lives, self-focused, ruled by fear, anger, or other debilitating emotions that imprison us. That is how struggles remain unresolved. In the past, this is the place where we spun our wheels until we felt exhausted and unhappy.

It is silly to believe that we are victims who need protection, that the other person is out to get us, but often we find ourselves falling into that bottomless well. Only darkness, isolation, and unhappiness exist there.

If we are operating with mental and emotional stress, we need to be kind and own our state, without judgment.

It is time to proceed to step two with conscious awareness.

STEP TWO: CHOOSE WHO YOU WANT TO BE

By pausing and being introspective, we ask:

- What is my intent? Who is the person I want to be?
- Do I want to continue to feel contracted and stressed, OR would I rather feel connected, at ease, and at peace?
- What stories keep me from seeing with clarity and joy?
- What thoughts keep my heart from being activated, even feeling generous?

This self-scrutiny establishes radical truth in the moment. It immediately calls us forth to take ownership of what we value and stand for. Being established in our power to choose is not focusing on what the other person is doing or not doing. It underscores instead that we make preferences about who we want to be with others. These are the most critical decisions to make.

These choices determine the tenor and success of our connection with another person. Choice shapes our lives. When we choose an open heart, filled with friendship and caring, it is like drinking in a day of sunshine after weeks of overcast gloom.

In a way, what the other person is doing doesn't even matter. He or she has simply offered us an opportunity to see ourselves in another light. In this person's form, the world stands before us one more time to reconfirm our commitment to who we want to be and what impact we want to make.

No matter what the circumstances, we can make a conscious choice for a better state. Even if we want the world to affirm how injured we are, we are still powerful, in charge, able to choose. What we cling to are stories that rob us of clarity and joy. Choosing a higher path might feel difficult to do. However, our serenity depends on us choosing our pure heart.

The moment to choose is now. Who will I be? What is my choice?

Assuming you choose to maintain a clear, steady state, let's get past any reactive thoughts and actions that have surfaced. You could hear my mind chatter during the project meeting described above. I had put up a wall to defend myself.

When we feel pain or dissent, there are frequently some thoughts—about the other person or about ourselves—that produce a shield. This defense is smog-like; it keeps us from seeing clearly. It hinders access to our peaceful heart. You can understand from the thoughts that bubbled up in my mind that I was in full-on resist-and-defend mode. The best action for me to take in a moment like this is to recall my intention and hold on to the choice that I made about the state I want to live from and maintain. That decision becomes leverage to move my mind to a gentler place.

It is a decisive moment when we turn away from the thoughts that were obstructing the relationship and move to a steadier heart and mind space. We step toward harmony and productivity. Making that choice, we are already in a better place. Step three will help make the shift.

STEP THREE: CENTER YOURSELF IN YOUR HEART

To take this step, we need to declutter our mind by pausing and calmly taking several quiet, slow, deep breaths in and out of our heart. As we breathe, make the commitment to step toward openness, toward kindheartedness—spaciousness. Relaxing into our breath, we can release and ease any physical tension. The sheer act of peaceful heart-breathing allows us to experience more connection to ourselves and the solid earth below. Instead of being driven by spiraling thoughts, we settle into our bodies in the present moment. We might even feel the clothes on our backs or the air on our skin or experience the fragrance of scents around us. We become more grounded.

Now we are ready to move deeper into step three; this will solidify our stance. Let's anchor the spaciousness we created with the breath by recalling a heartfelt connection, a moment in time when you were most truly yourself.

We have a plethora of beautiful moments—happy, free moments when our heart feels joy and is full of friendship and camaraderie. Recreate that space now—bring your mind and heart to one special memory. Choose one happy moment that currently seems most vivid and available. Breathe into the experience, and breathe it into you. Bathe in the delight of this experience until it feels alive inside. It is the key to unlock you from the prison of defensive thoughts. Embrace this wonderful memory fully.

Remembrance fills us to overflowing, like wonder sweeps through us when seeing a resplendent rainbow. Carry the fresh inner state with you as you continue with step four.

STEP FOUR: CONSIDER THE SITUATION WHOLEHEARTEDLY

Once we have arrived at step four, with our heart revitalized, we can consider the situation from a new vantage point. This is the step in the Japanese aesthetic of gold-mending. Just as we take special care with a child who is crying, we want to be generous, gentle, and kind as we look deeper. Our success depends on us genuinely exploring with clear perception and right understanding. True discernment is the ability to judge well from the stillness of our heart. By doing so, we can see what eluded us previously.

> If you look for the truth outside yourself,
> it gets farther and farther away.
> Today, walking alone,
> I meet him everywhere I step.
> He is the same as me,
> yet I am not him.
> Only if you understand it in this way
> will you merge with the way things are.
> Tung-shan (807–869)
> from *The Enlightened Heart*, 37

We can begin by appreciating that the other person is also struggling. We can expand our reality to include how the other person longs for harmony, just as we do. With honesty, we can look inside our heart to see what we have previously neglected. And once we allow ourselves to experience their humanity, our thinking shifts. We can begin to see the situation from their perspective:

- How does the struggle look and feel to the person?
- How have I been unwilling to see them and their concerns?
- Might I have missed seeing their good intentions?
- How might I be inviting something different than what I want?

○ What needs to shift in me? How could I help things go better between us?

Considering the other person's point of view gives us more information than when we were self-concerned. Our heart is more available from this inner reflection. Kintsugi helps imperfection mature into golden love, no longer needing to hide flaws, failure, or shame. When we honor what our heart whispers, we create connection and nonjudgmental intimacy. We heal the separation inside our mind and heart. We become present with what is—a stronger, more resilient version of ourselves being gold-mended.

We are now able to ask questions to consider our combined situation and resolve the uncomfortable circumstance. How can we best move forward? What might work for both of us? In asking these questions, we move from seeing ourselves on opposite sides of a situation, wanting to win or be right. We shift from a position of self-interest. We open into a caring perspective. The person now begins to matter to us. We soften, not in a powerless, "giving in" kind of way, but in an inclusive, "we both matter" kind of way. We stay connected with the other person while being responsible for our own state.

In my meeting, I could see how my reactive thoughts came from an unwillingness to care, open, listen, and understand. I was not connected to my heart. I might even have been nursing negative thoughts and feelings about this person or the project. I wouldn't be able to see through those walls. Also, I had in my mind a plan that I wanted. All these opinions spinning in my head created insensitivity.

Pondering the questions helped me to relax. I could see how the person I struggled against had planned out the event in detail to feel more at ease and make sure to complete every item. He had good intentions. He felt deeply responsible for the project's success. I saw how he needed to stay focused on the list to be productive while staying calm and collected. Instead of offering support as a team member, I had created stress for everyone.

From this more neutral, responsible, and inclusive perspective, I came to appreciate him. It was easy for me to choose to support his agenda. It now felt uncomplicated—like the right thing to do. What was interesting to me was that he became less rigid, more connected and collaborative, when I stopped resisting.

Once we move from a self-focused view to a "we" outlook, whatever the choice—whether to agree or disagree, participate or not—we will be able to respond with kindness and resolve tension. "We" is found in the heart—as a perpetual flame. Sincere openness will connect us to the flame quickly.

STEP FIVE: CREATE A GENEROUS-SPIRITED OPTION

In my example, once I returned to my heart, I chose to support who I previously had called the self-assigned leader; however, that is only one choice I could have made. Another choice could have been to breathe at the outset, be present, and truly listen to his needs and concerns. I might have been available instead of being blind.

Another choice: I could review his list with him and care about the importance he attributed to it. My acknowledgment could have eased the discussion. Once he felt heard, I might have added options—asked to share an alternative plan. Or I might have taken the approach to assure him that I could manage several items in a way that would be supportive, benefit our goal, and complete the project. From a "we" perspective, there are so many options that come to mind.

It is not so important what we choose to do. What is crucial is how alive our heart is with the person. That is such an important concept, it bears repeating: It is not so important what we choose to do. What is crucial is how alive our heart is with the person. When the stance of "we both matter" becomes more important than the outcome, being right, or winning, we step into creativity. Solutions naturally occur.

Each time we reach the space of "we" as a focus, new ways of seeing become possible. Internally reshaped, we complement the moment and the person. We naturally become more generous-spirited. Our final undertaking is to choose a peace-filled option, one that doesn't push against the other person like I was initially doing in my mind and heart. Our success lies in making a choice that honors our cooperation.

Once chosen, we summon up the courage it takes to follow through, to act with compassion for both of us. It takes one decision to change a struggle. My peaceful heart invites peacefulness.

Who will I be? That decision is up to me.

PERFECT FREEDOM

Imagine perfect freedom, where joyous laughter dances—
where estrangement and judgment are exchanged
for oneness.

Like the generous sun
shines on all without partiality,
receive others with open-spirited, warmhearted acceptance.

Collapse the walls of separation—
release differences,
grace every adversary with respect.

Spread the goodness of your radiant heart.
Wherever love is needed
impart warm affection, mutual esteem,
transcendent bliss.

CHAPTER 17
Stop-Struggling Formula for Success

When bumping heads with another person, we might notice the thought, "if only they would change" bubble up in our minds. In a moment like this, we forget that *change* is an inside job that we need to undertake. The efficacy of the relationship depends on us genuinely contemplating.

> *There's a monk there who will never give you advice, but only a question. I sought him out. "I am a parish priest," I said. "I'm here on retreat. Could you give me a question?"*
>
> *"Ah, yes," he answered. "My question is, 'What do they need?'"*
>
> *I came away disappointed. I spent a few hours with the question, writing out answers, but finally I went back to him.*
>
> *"Excuse me. Perhaps I didn't make myself clear. Your question has been helpful, but I wasn't so much interested in thinking about my apostolate during this retreat. Rather I wanted to think seriously about my own spiritual life. Could you give me a question for my own spiritual life?"*
>
> *"Ah, I see. Then my question is, 'What do they REALLY need?'"*
>
> from *Tales of a Magic Monastery*

We are all longing for connection. When we offer the safety of love, we can have relationships full of respect, serenity, success, and satisfaction. It is a beautiful gift we give ourselves and others. These steps lead to success.

1. Check your mental and emotional state.
   a. Pause.
   b. Notice thoughts and feelings.
   c. Proceed to the next step with conscious awareness.

2. Choose who you want to be.
   a. What is my intent? Who is the person I want to be?
   b. Do I want to continue to feel contracted and stressed OR feel connected, at ease, and at peace?
   c. What stories do I invest in that prevent seeing with clarity and joy?
   d. What thoughts keep my heart from being generous?

3. Center yourself in your heart. Step wholly into peace.
   a. Heart-breathe calmly. Relax into each slow, deep inhalation and exhalation, releasing any physical tension.
   b. Experience being connected to the solid earth below you; feel the air on your skin and the clothes on your back.
   c. Recall a heartfelt connection with a free, happy, or peaceful moment. As it becomes alive inside, embrace and anchor yourself in it fully.

4. Consider the situation wholeheartedly. Acknowledge what has been unseen.
   a. Appreciate that you have both been struggling.
   b. Know that the other person longs for an end to tension, just as you do.

c.   Tell the whole truth. Explore the situation through these lenses.

Truth be told:

i.   How does this struggle look and feel to the person?

ii.   How have you not been willing to see them and their concerns?

iii.   How might you have missed seeing their good intention?

iv.   How might you be inviting something different than what you want?

v.   What needs to shift in you? How could you help things go better?

5. Create a generous-spirited option. Make "we" indispensable.

a.   Summon up the courage it takes to choose wisely.

b.   Make a choice that honors your precious heart.

c.   Follow through. Act with compassion for both of you.

HELPFUL TIPS

Life will continue to give us opportunities to grow healthier in our relationships with others. Even if others do not change, you will be honoring your values and experiencing less struggle.

Uncomfortable moments will occur; that is the nature of things. Practice by taking one step at a time from wherever you are now. This action will naturally propel you forward and prepare you for future interactions.

To thrive, clearly commit to the state of how you wish to live. Hold firmly to that intention, even when earthquake-like shocks happen in a relationship. The nurturance of your decision will direct your life and your moment-to-moment responses.

Notice where you are doing well and where you might improve. Remember, life takes practice. It is important to keep refreshing your commitment.

To become skilled, schedule actual times when you will perform the success formula in its entirety. You can do that while reflecting on a difficult encounter and progress through the steps, discovering new information and new choices.

Each time you practice, you are

1. understanding yourself better;
2. firmly establishing the way of being in which you want to live;
3. dissolving old patterns of thinking, defending, reacting; and
4. creating neural pathways of respectful possibilities.

Practice the formula until it feels deeply integrated—until it is in your bones. Over time, you will notice that the steps will become natural to you. Then these five main steps can be your companions to guide you in difficult times.

Check your mental and emotional state.
Choose who you want to be.
Center yourself in your heart.
Consider the situation wholeheartedly.
Create a generous-spirited option and act.

After a short while, you will get good at noticing a thought that drags you down. You will come to recognize when your spirit dips. That is an excellent time to pause. Perhaps at that moment, you cannot shift your heart and mind because the matter is too important to you. If that is the case, resolve to stop building the story and defense structure any further. Know for this moment that you are not prepared to act with clarity, kindness, and integrity. In time, with patience and resolve, you will be able to respond respectfully in even the most challenging situations.

Become dedicated to the state from which you would like to engage.

Remember the five C's—Check in, Choose, Center, Consider, and Create. There will be times you'll need to communicate something difficult to someone. With kindness and respect, everything goes better. You can even be quite firm while being respectful. With steadfastness, you will improve your relationships. You are up for the task—this practice will grant you freedom. Your heart and mind will thank you.

It takes one decision to change a struggle.
Practicing will strengthen your capacity to choose and live well.

EVER-PRESENT ONE

Imagine how selfless Generosity
gifts you audience,
holds your trembling mind when you are scared,
serves your sacred heart in ways seen and unseen,
provides all you need.

Like a mighty river returning to the ocean,
leave behind fear, resistance, timidity, title.
Reclaim your rightful self—confident and lionhearted
free your heart to flow effortlessly and swiftly to others.
Become the ocean.

CHAPTER 18
Cultivate Enduring Calm

Perhaps there are many places in our lives where a spirit of calm may not be present. Those places invite us to expand into more love, compassion, and mercy for situations, for ourselves, and the people in our lives.

At a New Year's Day retreat, I heard the phrase "enduring calm" and longed to experience that state. The phrase enchanted me. Since it was so soothing to my ears, I repeated it like a mantra on silent walks in the garden. This tranquil phrase kept echoing in my heart, urging me to come home and rest.

I felt sure that this was more than business as usual. I just kept following its resonant sound to a place beyond my understanding, to a serene way of living. It put my heart's love front and center.

Great teachers can help us on the journey. Dr. C. Terry Warner, in his book *Bonds That Make Us Free*, expertly leads us from bonds of anguish to bonds of love. Here is one of his statements that pierces my heart: "The humanity we find in others becomes our own, measured exactly. That is how human beings achieve depth of soul."

I respect Dr. Warner, and his statement puts me on notice. It wakes me from a daze, stops me in what I am doing, and requires me to look closely at how I am in relation to each person in my life.

Where is it that I do not let a person off the hook? How am I not allowing people into my heart? What is churning inside me? What excuse do I give to dismiss my responsibility?

I ponder many levels of meaning: "*The humanity we find in others becomes our own, measured exactly.*" The judgments I make and the love and compassion I deny a person are how I see and value myself. I lack mercy and compassion.

HONEST CONSIDERATION

Let's travel together to genuinely see the anguish we cause when we don't catch a seed of hurt before it festers. Our mind becomes engrossed in a world of justification for the way we are thinking and feeling. Holding tight to pain and refusing to see the other person causes the story inside our mind to intensify and leads to agitation. What we assign as the causes of our hurt and pain seem reasonable and valid to us. However, they are unrelated to discovering humanity in the other person.

THE TALMUD TELLS US: "WE DO NOT SEE THINGS AS THEY ARE; WE SEE THEM AS WE ARE."

This actuality is why we need to be crystal clear about how our mind and heart are engaged. Otherwise, each time we feel disrespected, hurt, jealous, upstaged, frustrated, or ignored, we can get caught in a quandary of thoughts, feelings, and behaviors.

In our heart and mind, we walk away from the person. We begin to harbor feelings of righteousness and resentment. Our self-focused narrative, bolstered by feelings, leaves no recognition that there might be a different story, another perspective. Discernment has left the premises. Our pride tells us all sorts of things about how right we are and how we deserve respect.

How can we expect a person to feel kindly toward us when our attitude offends with blame and superiority? How can we imagine a person could be loving toward us when we are so enamored of our rationalizations? How can we expect a person to be honest and forthcoming with us when we act so saintly? How can the atmosphere that our enmity creates resolve anything?

We have pulled away and want the person punished. We have not taken responsibility for our contribution to the pain or even for our relationship with them. We need to peel away the layers of encrustation that bury the purity of love waiting, ready to be experienced.

In the movie *The Mahabharata*, a famous epic of ancient India, Lord Krishna gives the sage advice, "In reality, where there is love, there is no desire. Love is born out of humility, whereas desire is born out of pride."

Now is a moment of choice. We might take the familiar route further into the depths of feelings and their subsequent thoughts and reactions. That direction can be almost automatic. With awareness and intention, we can choose the lionhearted route to solve our problems.

FRESH START

It is all right to regret not being the best friend, coworker, neighbor, or relative we could have been—no reason to worry. Instead, right now we can establish a feeling of friendliness and optimism deep in our heart. Our mind has served us to the best of our ability. Making unproductive choices in the past has helped us to learn better ways, a better path to enter our heart sooner. Within our reach are peace and enduring calm.

All of us, both people we know and those we do not know, are on the same journey, wishing to be content and free, at peace, feeling loved and lovable.

I invite you to be with yourself in a very gentle, friendly way. Be warmhearted with yourself. Experience the light that shines in your heart. If you do not experience light, recognize bright energy sparking within you, allowing your eyes to move, your heart to pulsate. Feel assured that you are loved.

Wrap your arms around yourself tenderly, as you would hold a scared child in your arms. Make space for feelings of warmth and kindness to arise. Be full of care; let self-compassion emerge; and allow yourself to embrace, without judgment, your capacity for offering mercy and compassion. Your loving acceptance of yourself is a healing balm.

Even now, follow the gentle movement of your breath as it rises and falls inside your rib cage. Slip into a slow, rhythmic breath to relax your mind and ease your heart. Enjoy the feeling of letting go into this present moment as you release within.

Welcome to your heart a loved one, someone you dearly cherish. Feel the deep connection and joy you have for this incredible person in your life.

Now, remember a time during your relationship with them when they, without a trace of selfishness, forgave you—for something small or grand. Recapture the feelings you felt. Perhaps it was reprieve or gratefulness. When forgiveness happens, both hearts relax, feel calm, and exclaim "yes," affirming how everything feels right again, connected.

Reflect on how they are human and have struggled in a similar way to forgive a person in their life. Fill your entire being with tenderness and compassion. From your grateful heart send this loved one gratitude and wishes for their happiness and peace. Linger in this kindhearted space for a while. And enjoy a fountain of love and connection flowing between you.

Maintain the experience of this person in your heart. Also, take your loved one's virtual hand; ask them to stand beside you and help you make the next steps toward peace.

Give yourself space to experience pure goodness in your own and your loved one's hearts.

You are now prepared to be courageous. Focus your attention on the area of your heart and imagine several slow, deep breaths flowing in and out of your heart. Choose one person that needs your mercy and compassion. Form a mental image of them. Perceive the light that shines in them. Open to the goodness in their heart.

Lovingly sip from a fountain of compassion that flows in your heart. Look with soft, kind eyes to see how you might be blind to their pain and suffering. Wonder what your judgment might be creating for them. Let the truth about their heart write itself upon your heart. Discover their humanity, your humanity.

Take your time to appreciate this person. Allow even one drop of compassion or understanding to multiply and fill a golden pond of love in your heart. In this sacred space, open to expansive energy.

True forgiveness graciously opens a door
for you to walk through—
welcomes you with reverence,
takes your hand
sensing the tearing in your heart.

Compassionate,
unconditional
forgiveness looks with you anew
at disappointment and separateness
from another.

Allow mercy and sincerity to merge
like the sacred confluence of two rivers.
Expand your vision,
let kindheartedness blossom,
offer pure sentiments of respect and love.

Mother Teresa lived her life knowing the truth: "It is not what we do; it is how much love we put in the doing. It is not what we give; it is how much love we put in the giving."

Do not delay; go to this person. Be clothed in humility and kindness; speak truthfully from your heart to theirs. With love, you can care for both of you simultaneously.

WE WILL BE HAPPY WHEN WE ARE INVESTED IN OTHER PEOPLE'S HAPPINESS

Breathe easily. Seeing from your heart with clearer vision sets you free. Perhaps you need to ponder compassion in your relationships further. Take the time you need to contemplate. In the ancient Sanskrit language, the word for patience also means forgiveness. Have no worries. Freedom and happiness are right around the bend. With practice, you can achieve enduring calm.

You have been pondering deeply; you have been welcoming yourself to your heart more and more, recapturing oneness. Return once more to Dr. Warner's quotation: "The humanity we find in others becomes our own, measured exactly. That is how human beings achieve depth of soul." Our heart, mind, and soul rejoice and thrive when tethered together. Trust the unfolding of love in you; it is all-wise and knows the way to enduring calm.

All the relationships encountered in life offer one question to ponder—How much do you love?

Relax; seek love so your heart can experience its full bloom. Resolve never to cover it over. Then it will radiate through your being to those you meet.

CHAPTER 19
The Sure Path

People often search for and want "the prize" –the perfect remedy, the wonderful partner, the new car, winning the lottery. We think fulfilling our desires will bring us happiness. There is no need to push away, or get rid of what feels like "not enough." The tension that comes from unfulfilled desire, fear, worry, or working hard actually blinds us. We fail to appreciate what is already ours. Our dissatisfaction colors our way of being in the world.

He asked me what I was looking for.

"Frankly," I said, "I'm looking for the Pearl of Great Price."

He slipped his hand into his pocket, drew it out, AND GAVE IT TO ME. It was just like that! I was dumbfounded. Then I began to protest: "You don't want to give it to me! Don't you want to keep it for yourself? But . . ."

When I kept this up, he said finally, "Look, is it better to have the Pearl of Great Price, or to give it away?"

Well, now I have it. I don't tell anyone. From some there would just be disbelief and ridicule. "You, you have the Pearl of Great Price? Hah!" Others would be jealous, or someone might steal it.

Yes, I do have it. But there's the question—"Is it better to have it, or to give it away?"

How long will that question rob me of my joy?

from Tales of a Magic Monastery

Oh dear, how challenging our internal conflicts can make life. It is crucial to be vigilant and see what is occurring. My own experience taught me many valuable lessons.

A long while back, I twisted my leg so severely that I injured my left foot and ankle. The pain was excruciating. Beyond the pain, I was greatly inconvenienced. It was difficult doing some of the simplest tasks. I grumbled. I had to slow down and even eliminate some activities.

Even though I felt frustrated and angry, this hardship caused me to think about how spoiled I am and act, and how I take my physical well-being for granted. I am used to coming and going as I please.

Perhaps you can understand. Maybe you have had a disturbing set of circumstances and found yourself in a grumpy or ill-tempered state. Like me, your disposition and mood might change from friendly to being self-absorbed and miserable.

When I was disabled and in my slower, challenged, hobbling state, I became aware of people I hadn't seen before—people with disabilities far more critical than mine. Unlike some of the people I saw, my inconveniences were temporary. I would heal and be free. I reflected on how being a curmudgeon was a choice I made that was blown way out of proportion. My crankiness blinded me.

Living with the nuisance from my injury opened my eyes and led me to contemplate who I was being and how I was behaving. Being cranky was a choice. Pondering showed me how I needed to make a better choice.

Whenever I caught my thoughts drifting to complaints, I started settling into being more relaxed and less frustrated. Now, slipping out of victimhood, I was gracious when someone opened a door for me or offered to get my groceries. People were making my life easier; I was grateful. Some people made me smile or laugh. With a lighter heart, I experienced appreciation.

Stepping into my grateful heart mysteriously turned the fear and anxiety of night into day. Rather than consoling myself about my misfortune, I became cheerful once again and probably much more pleasant to be around.

A miracle happened. My injury still slowed me down; however, my mind was thinking clearly. My internal conversations shifted from self-critical and complaining to a voice that had kindness and warmth for myself and others. I was happy again rather than sullen. I still hobbled; however, I was not making everyone's day miserable.

With gratitude, I began to trust and stopped demanding life to do it my way—to fulfill my desires. Out of gratitude, I became generous and gave people what they needed without needing anything in return. This shift of focus transformed my energy to making everyone else's day great. It feels so good to make someone else happy.

It makes no difference how big or infinitesimal the gift or actions are. What truly matters is how our heart is connected to the person while offering it. See how many people your heart can uplift.

- o What is a kind thing you could say to someone?
- o How could you spend even a moment or two of quality time with someone?
- o What is the smallest thing you could do for someone without them knowing it was you?

When I offered a kindness that only I knew of, satisfaction washed over me, and recognition of my good fortune blossomed.

My mishap brought to light many understandings about a grateful heart that I am practicing. Here are twelve experiences and conclusions I came to that I would like to share. Whether your pain is physical or emotional, if any of these are helpful to you, please make them your own.

- Gratitude is one fantastic remedy for any misery, small or large. Keep its healing balm with you always.
- It is *not* possible to be upset and grateful at the same time. Be generous and acknowledge others.
- When something (like noticing a beautiful flower, a friend reaching out, someone paying for your hot beverage) wakes you from your stupor, enjoy it. Savor it and be grateful.
- If things aren't going well or times are challenging, make it your practice to pause (obviously a good help in itself) and begin experiencing kindness. Did you rest last evening? Did you look at the sky today? Have a little food for your stomach? Have water to drink? Wonder who are the multitudes of people that, because of them, your cup is full?
- If you feel past hope or too far away from your heart, you can start with respect for your eyes, ears, feet, hands, and brain function; add other body parts as well. Think about how you take your body for granted. What would life be like without one of your senses or limbs? Even allow yourself to be amazed by what a sense, an internal organ, or a limb provides for you. Who would you be without it?
- Drink in nature in all its wonder, with its beautiful array of colors. Fling open your heart to it all.
- When you settle a little more inside and feel relaxed, reflect on the blessings that are in your life, even ones that you might

not usually recall. Don't just think about them. Instead, truly experience your deep appreciation for each one.

o Make effort because it is the right thing to do; dissolve the expectation of being acknowledged. Expectations get in the way of being grateful and enjoying the moment.

o Give thanks for all the little things in life. Everything is a gift and deserves your honor and protection.

o Gratefulness grows with practice and often gives rise to humility. Be surprised.

o In being thankful, you will come to trust in life and how it is utterly gratuitous.

o Happiness is not an accident; gratitude is the sure path.

Startled by wild applause and roused from slumber,
you thrill to memories of generous hearts throughout life.

Recalling wondrous connections and celebrations,
your heart bursts with gratitude—
not in a loud, hooray kind of way,
more like a fall-to-your-knees tender genuflection.

Fastened to humility and resolve,
feel privileged to walk the earth.

Welcome every shard and pebble in your shoe
not as punishment or merely pain
but jewels of immense love and caring—
passports to a life of confidence, resilience, jubilation.

Appreciate! Appreciate! Appreciate! Notice your great good fortune.
Be free from feelings of lack; fill with peace and contentment. Allow

gratitude to become your way of being. Feel happy; be generous. Bless others.

May your life always overflow with grateful blessings.

Contemplate this question: Do you lose the Pearl of Great Price when you give it away?

May you experience peace.

CHAPTER 20
Traveling with Hope

Wrapped in the warmth of love, your precious heart unfailingly lights the path to a life of extraordinary joy, peace, prosperity.

Love it all.
Savor sweet oneness.
Cherish all your relationships.
Listen with your heart to others' hearts.
Express tender compassion toward others.
Throw open the floodgates to expansive love.

Smile.
Forgive perpetually.
Accept human frailty.
Laugh until your sides ache.
Appreciate, Appreciate, Appreciate
Enjoy a sense of humor toward yourself.
Bless it all—be grateful for the wisdom gained.

Be Happy.
Embrace surprises.
Allow your mind stillness.
Sink into blissful silence within.
Bask in your heart's radiant brilliance.
Attend to the quiet whispers in your heart.
Honor your pure, perfect, phenomenal mind.
Relax into the peace your precious breath offers.
Brighten every thought and word with molten gold.
Is it kind? Is it true? Is it beneficial? Is it the right time?

APACHE BLESSING

May the sun
bring you energy by day;

May the moon
softly restore you by night;

May the rain
wash away your worries;

May the breeze
blow new strength into your being;

May you walk gently
through the world
and know its beauty
all the days of your life.

References and Recommended Reading

The poems in this book, unless otherwise indicated, are written by Nancy A Smyth.

Nancy learned the Navajo chant while visiting her Navajo friends in Window Rock, Arizona, and the Apache Blessing while living in the Southwest.

Albom, Mitch. *Tuesdays with Morrie*. New York: Random House, 1997.

Berger, Barbara. *Grandfather Twilight*. New York: Philomel Books, 1984.

Brain Pickings: https://www.brainpickings.org/2015/10/21/telling-is-listening-ursula-k-le-guin-communication/

Carroll, Jim. "Me. We." *Jim Carroll's Blog*, April 24, 2015, https://www.jimcarrollsblog.com/blog/2015/4/3/mewe.

Chidvilasananda, Gurumayi. *Sadhana of the Heart: A Collection of Talks on Spiritual Life*. South Fallsburg, NY: SYDA Foundation, 2006.

Childre, Doc Lew, and Howard Martin. *The HeartMath Solution: The Institute of HeartMath's Revolutionary Program for Engaging the Power of the Heart's Intelligence*. New York: Harper Collins, 2000.

Chopra, Deepak, Kafatos, Menas, Kak, Subhash, Tanzi, Rudolph E., and Theise, Neil. "Can Brain Science Explain Experience?" *HuffPost*, May 5, 2014.

Dalai Lama, His Holiness, and Cutler, Howard C. *The Art of Happiness, 10th Anniversary Edition*. New York: Riverhead Books, 1998.

Gu, Master Mingtong. *Wisdom Healing (Zhineng) Qigong: Cultivating Wisdom and Energy for Health, Healing and Happiness*. Mingtong Gu, 2011.

Jinpa, Thupten. *A Fearless Heart: How the Courage to Be Compassionate Can Transform Our Lives*. New York: Penguin Random House, 2015.

Kabir: https://isalove.org/writings/kabir/kabir1.html

Kahane, Adam. *Power and Love: A Theory and Practice of Social Change*. San Francisco: Berrett-Koehler Publishers, 2010.

Make-A-Wish Arizona: https://wish.org/arizona/our-stories

Mitchell, Stephen (Ed.). *An Anthology of Sacred Poetry*. New York: HarperCollins Publishers, 1989.

Muktananda, Swami. *From the Finite to the Infinite*. Fallsburg, NY: SYDA Foundation, 1994.

Murthy, Vivek H. *Together: The Healing Power of Human Connection in a Sometimes Lonely World*. New York: HarperCollins, 2020.

Nassim Haramein: The Connected Universe | Nassim Haramein | TEDxUCSD https://www.youtube.com/watch?v=xJsl_klqVh0

Pearson, Carol Lynn. *The Lesson: A Fable for Our Times*. Layton, UT: Gibbs Smith, 1998.

Pflueger, Lynne, and Wenninger, Michael. *What Mary Says: Jin Shin Jiutsu*. JSJ Inc., 1997.

Ram Dass and Paul Gorman, *How Can I Help*. New York: Alfred A. Knopf, 1985

Sardello, Robert, and Sanders-Sardello, Cheryl. *Silence: The Mystery of Wholeness*. Berkeley: Goldenstone Press, 2008.

Scharmer, C. Otto. *Leading from the Emerging Future: From Ego-System to Eco-System Economies*. San Francisco: Barret-Koehler Publishers, 2013.

Shah, Indries. *The Exploits of the Incomparable Mulla Nasrudin.* London: E.P. Dutton & Co., 1972.

Sorensen, Eric Kristen. *New Tales of Nasrudin.* Lincoln, NE: iUniverse, 2006.

Stevens, Christina. *Love.* Carlsbad, CA: Hay House, 2014.

Subramaniam, Hamala. *Mahabharata.* Mumbai: Bharatiya Vida Bhavan, 1985.

The Arbinger Institute. *The Anatomy of Peace: Resolving the Heart of Conflict.* Oakland, CA: Berrett-Koehler Publishers, 2006.

Theophane the Monk. *Tales of a Magic Monastery.* The Crossroad Publishing Company, 1988.

Warner, C. Terry. *Bonds That Make Us Free.* Salt Lake City, UT: Shadow Mountain, 2001.

Wikipedia: "Health Effects of Noise." Wikipedia, Wikimedia Foundation, 2021, https://en.wikipedia.org/wiki/Health_effects_from_noise.

Acknowledgments

I have immense gratitude for—

My parents giving birth to me and helping me discover my calling in the world.

My dear children, who constantly lightened my heart; as they matured, I matured—they taught me to enjoy life and helped me put forth the effort to become a better person.

John, for seeing I needed help and taking me to yoga every week, even when it probably was not his cup of tea.

Beautiful grandchildren embarking on wondrous lives to add their brilliance to the planet.

The many superb teachers from whom I learned a better way to live.

My business partner, Sharon walking with me through many years as a friend and coach.

All my coaches, who challenged and encouraged me to stretch and see more than I could see.

My precious sister, Patt, and my dearest friends that have traveled through time with me, offering so much love and faith.

My clients, who continue to teach me courage, persistence, and patience.

And most importantly, thank you, dear Lord, for this blessed life. Thank you for leading me to my Guru, who has given me everything. I am no longer who I thought I was, fearful, small, and insignificant. Thank you.

I honor those who encouraged my writing, putting into form what I treasure.

I also offer my thanks to you, the reader who walked with me.

About the Author

Middle child, first girl, smart and shy, cautious and fearful, not like other girls, loved playing baseball, riding bikes, skating, climbing trees, wanted to be a priest, loved art, a whiz at math.

High school National Honor Society, couldn't afford college, worked full-time, learned the banking business, saved money, went to night school for four years, OSU for one year, didn't receive a degree.

Married: two awesome, fun sons eleven months apart—talented, smart as whips; became foster parents for infants, then adopted a baby daughter. She was completely blind in both eyes, cataracts removed, still severely visually impaired, couldn't lift her head or move her arms or legs at age one. Helped her and other brain-injured children. She is quite remarkable and lives independently with her dog.

Touched on meditation at my convent high school, delved into its practice in 1969, and have continued since then. I love teaching meditation.

Since my youth, my core value has been love; building and sustaining relationships is central to my life—work to know and understand the truth about myself and others; compassion is also central.

Received certification in counseling and intensive training in yoga and other body-work disciplines and healing techniques.

Four-year apprenticeship in the art of physical, mental, spiritual, and emotional healing with Mike Valenzuela—Aztec Indian medicine man.

Training and experiences with Native Americans and other cultural groups studying energy healing.

Met my Guru in 1990, lived in the ashram in India 1998 through 1999.

Graduated from an ICF-accredited coaching program and completed a year-long leadership program.

Invited by The Arbinger Institute in 2003 to create a worldwide coaching program; co-contributor to their bestseller, *The Anatomy of Peace*; continue to train and offer executive coaching for the Institute.

Co-Founded Two Wise Women, a coaching and training business that published *Chocolate or Lunch: How Choices Impact Relationships* in 2015.

Currently contribute as a thought leader, inspirational speaker, trainer, and Master Certified Coach.

nancysmyth624@gmail.com

Lightning Source UK Ltd.
Milton Keynes UK
UKHW020858040821
388259UK00011B/2586